William ||||||||||||||| D1256162 rr-nister

THE GREAT SALVATION

by

P. H. WELSHIMER

Minister at First Christian Church, Canton, Ohio

INTRODUCTION

By the Editor of THE LOOKOUT

The author of this book not only writes sermons and preaches sermons—his life is a sermon in itself. P. H. Welshimer measures up to the admonition in Ephesians 4: 1b—"Walk worthy of the vocation wherewith ye are called."

He is the kind of man who, had he chosen business as a career, would have gained position as head of some great corporation by sheer energy and organizational ability. If he had chosen science, law, medicine, politics, finance, or any other secular field, his success would have won him fame.

Instead, he is notable for his achievements in that greatest of all vocations, the Christian ministry. During the more than half a century that he has been its minister, First Christian Church at Canton, Ohio, has become the largest such church of record, with a membership numbering well up into the thousands. At conventions, conferences, and other meetings throughout the nation he has been heard by multitudes. Countless others know him through his writing. He is one of the best-known preachers in America today.

What is the secret of his success? I believe it is not only his fidelity to the appeal of the apostle, but also his response to the pull of the people. "P. H." is a people's preacher. He enlists the hearts and minds of men of high and low degree. The sermons in this book are of the type that have made him and his work a success.

GUY P. LEAVITT

INDEX

DEDICATION

To my grandchildren
Paula and Mark Welshimer

"THE GREAT SALVATION"

Hebrews 2: 3

"How shall we escape, if we neglect so great salvation?" (Hebrews 2: 3). In this text Paul is calling the Hebrews to task for having neglected the great salvation. The superiority of the gospel over the law had not been thoroughly understood by the Jewish people. They still were glorying in the work of Moses, the lawgiver, placing him in a position superior to that of the Christ. Paul assures the Hebrews that God, who at different times and in various ways spoke to the fathers in the olden times by the prophets, now speaks through His Son "whom he hath appointed heir of all things, by whom also he made the worlds." Christ is introduced as being "the brightness of his glory, and the express image of his person" and that today He sits at the right hand of the "Majesty on high."

Christ was exalted as the Son of God and all the angels were commanded to worship Him. Christ is far above the angels who are ministering spirits. Christ is the only begotten Son of God, the one concerning whom all the prophets spoke. His name is above every name.

The salvation which Christ offers is known as "the great salvation." It overshadows the law and the old covenant. Paul admonished the Hebrews to give earnest heed to the things they had heard, lest at any time they would let them slip. Then comes the question, "If the word spoken by angels was stedfast, and every transgression and disobedience received a just recompense of re-

ward; how shall we escape, if we neglect so great salvation?"

We reject something that is offered us, and we neglect that which having been offered, we receive. A man
may reject a gift that is promised. He neglects that
which he has received. The Jews to whom Paul was
writing had accepted the Christ and had become identified with His body, the church. Now they are rapidly
fading away, following afar off, neglecting that which
they had received.

Paul comes with the question, "How shall we escape,
if we neglect so great salvation?"

In this sermon we are considering the great salvation.
It was a great salvation because it was an eternal salvation, not a temporal one. It is the salvation presented
in the gospel. The great salvation came not from the
reasonings of human beings, but it was that "faith once
for all delivered unto the saints." Before ascending to
the Father, Jesus told His disciples, who were to be His
ambassadors, to tarry in Jerusalem until they were endued with power from on high. He promised that He
would pray the Father, who would send to them the
Holy Spirit, which would guide them into all truth.
Those men went panoplied with power. They were for-
tified against the arguments and the attacks of the enemy. The great salvation was presented by the Son of
God. He is its author and the apostles were the individuals to whom the gospel message came through the agency
of the Holy Spirit. In the forty days of the sojourn of
Jesus with the disciples, between the resurrection morning and His ascension, we are told He talked with them
concerning many things pertaining to the kingdom.

On the day of the ascension of Jesus, He commissioned them. He ascended to the Father. They went to the upper room in Jerusalem and continued in prayer until Pentecost, fifty days after the resurrection.

From Pentecost those men went forward telling the world of "the great salvation." It was the great salvation because it was universal. "Whosoever shall call on the name of the Lord shall be saved." "Go ye into all the world and preach the gospel to every creature." "He that believeth and is baptized shall be saved; he that believeth not shall be damned."

It is the great salvation, for it is the only salvation offered to man. The law was nailed to the cross with Christ. It ended there. The gospel takes the place of the law. Christ overshadows Moses. In the long ago Moses said to the people, "The Lord thy God will raise up unto thee a Prophet from the midst of thee, of thy brethren, like unto me." God said to the disciples at the time He was transfigured at the conference held with Moses and Elias, "This is my beloved Son: hear him." The great salvation is simple and plain. There are many mysteries connected with godliness. There is no mystery associated with what man is to do in fulfilling the conditions of the great salvation. It is so simple that he who runs may read. The terms have been presented by God-called men who spoke in language that people could understand. No contradictions arose among the apostles in their preaching in that apostolic period.

The salvation was great because it was confirmed by miraculous power. The apostles had credentials which convinced the hearing world that the message was genuine, not man-made, not uncertain, but was a sincere word

of God. They wrought miracles which proved that God
was with them, and therefore they were reliable. The
words they spoke conveyed to the hearers the mind and
the plan of God. When an ambassador comes from the
British Isles, representing his country, to the United States,
he goes to Washington and presents his credentials. So,
likewise, the apostolic preachers had credentials when
they wrought miracles. Jesus came with credentials from
heaven. Nicodemus said to Him, "Rabbi, we know
that thou art a teacher come from God: for no man can do
these miracles that thou doest, except God be with him."

Many are much confused today as they listen to the
discordant voices claiming to present the truth of the
great salvation. The messages are not all alike. They
differ much in the steps to be taken by which forgiveness of sins is promised. They "do err, not knowing the
scriptures." The conflicting voices disturb many people. Jesus prayed that His disciples might be one in
their preaching in order that the world might believe
that God had sent Him.

The great salvation is free—"come . . . without money
and without price." It is the gift of God. His grace
is divine favor. "By grace are ye saved," which means
God offers salvation to all who will accept His Son, Jesus
the Christ, and comply with the conditions stipulated.
The great salvation can not be bought. It comes to men
in all stations and walks of life. God is no respecter of
persons. It is an inheritance vouchsafed to the children
of God.

The great salvation gives one the more abundant life.
Jesus said, "I am come that they might have life and . . .
have it more abundantly." It should not be considered a

fire escape. It is intended for the life now and here, and in its acceptance we are prepared for the life that continues beyond the death of the body. The peace for which the world yearns can be obtained only when the great salvation has been accepted by the people of the world. It makes of the world a great brotherhood. It constitutes one kingdom with Christ as the king; one great family where God is the Father, Christ the elder brother, and all believers adopted members in that family. Jesus said as He looked over sad Jerusalem, "Come unto me, all ye that labour and are heavy laden, and I will give you rest. Take my yoke upon you, and learn of me; for I am meek and lowly of heart: and ye shall find rest unto your souls."

The great salvation makes the world a better place in which to dwell. Years ago there was an island in the sea, not far from Holland, where the pirates resorted. They were disturbers of the peace, robbers of life. The government sent a young man by the name of Bok to that island. He transformed it. The pirates were driven out. Birds of the finest song and plumage were introduced to the island. Good people moved in and in time the island became like to a paradise of God. The man married. Little boys were born into his home. When death rapped at his door, he told the children of the work he had done, the purpose of his having come, and said to them that he came that the island might be made a beautiful place in which men could dwell. And he instructed them that wherever they went that should be their purpose in life. One of those boys was Edward Bok, who, with his mother, came to the United States. For twenty-six years he was editor of the *Ladies Home*

Journal, and he took as his purpose the making of the land in which he dwelt a fit place in which men could dwell. That was the purpose of the Christ and the ambassadors whom He sent forth. He gave to them the system, the good news, the power that would transform the lives of men and to help them make this old world a better place for men to dwell. Nothing can surpass the great salvation in this task.

The great salvation never fails when given the opportunity to run and be glorified. One goes to the Patent Office in Washington, D. C., and finds there patents have been granted on many implements of service which never are to be found in the field, factory, or home. One asks the question, Why are these not seen when they have been patented? And the reply is they worked fairly well in the model, but did not function in the practical affairs of everyday life. There are many theories, opinions, philosophies, that are brought forth for the advancement of men. In the last analysis they are merely words—words—words. They do not work. Not so with the great salvation—it works! We see it working all about us.

Some years ago a young man was called to preach in an evangelistic meeting in an Ohio town. In that town was a family consisting of the father, two little daughters, and a young son. They lived in an old ramshackle house down by the railroad. It was poorly furnished, the yard was decorated with tin cans. The little girls did their best in maintaining the home. The father was dissolute, spent much of his money for drink. The little girls and the little boy attended the evangelistic meeting. The invitation was extended and the girls came forward, confessing their faith in the Christ. A woman in that church with more vanity than religion, objected to these little girls becoming members of the church with which she was identified. The preacher stood his ground, baptized them and, before the meeting closed, had baptized the little boy and the father. They sang the last song, offered the last prayer, and the folk went home. The preacher went back to his pastorate. Some years went by. He had occasion to pass through that town again, and he stopped to call upon some friends. He inquired about the poor family. He was taken by a member who showed him the place of their habitation and gave this report: The father had now put on the habiliments of a respected, Christian manhood. He was the mayor of the town and an elder in the church. The little girls, grown to womanhood, were members of the choir, teachers in the Bible school, and had married young men who were active workers in the church. The little boy, now grown to young manhood, was a deacon in the church, president of Rotary, and the superintendent of a prosperous factory in the town. What brought about this change? Just one thing. It was that concerning which Paul said, "I am not ashamed of the gospel of Christ: for it is the power of God unto salvation to every one that believeth."

This is the only salvation that gives the promise of immortality. Christ said He was going to prepare a place for His disciples, and that He would return and receive them unto Himself. He said, "Because I live, ye shall live also." After a faithful service and an eventful life, as the shadows of the day of life were gathering, Paul, the great soldier of the cross wrote from his prison cell to Timothy, "I am now ready to be offered, and the time of my departure is at hand. I have fought a good fight, I have finished my course, I have kept the faith: henceforth there is laid up for me a crown of righteousness, which the Lord, the righteous judge, shall give me at that day: and not to me only, but unto all them also that love his appearing." This is the promise to all the faithful. All that a man has here on the earth does not give life, for "what shall it profit a man, if he shall gain the whole world, and lose his own soul?" Only by accepting the great salvation do we have any promise and any hope of entering into that rest that is promised to the people of God.

Hence, the question of Paul, "How shall we escape, if we neglect so great salvation?" It is offered us, but some reject it. Others accept and then neglect. One neglects the great salvation who is unconcerned, pursues the even tenor of his way, enjoys the life that now is, simply lives for the present day and, like the rich man in the Bible, wears fine linen and fairs sumptuously every day, but has no concern about his own soul and offers no helping hand to those in need who daily pass his gate.

The greatest task for the preacher today is to awaken people from their lethargy and to call them to repentance. It is true today as of old: "Except ye repent, ye shall all likewise perish."

One who has accepted the Christ, believing with all his heart that He is the only begotten Son of God, who repents of his sins, confesses his faith in the Christ, and is buried with Him in Christian baptism is then commanded to continue steadfastly in the apostles' doctrine,

in fellowship, in prayers and in the breaking of bread.
But if he neglects these things and fails to continue
working out his own salvation with fear and trembling,
he becomes neglectful of the only saving power known
to man.   One neglects the great salvation when he ceases
to be a worshiper in the church of the living God;
when he has no quiet hour wherein he may commune
with the heavenly Father; when he ceases to study and
to profit by the written Word; when he takes no interest in the affairs of the kingdom of God; when he ceases
to feed the hungry, visit the sick, care for the despondent and make himself a friend to man.   To enter the
kingdom of heaven one must do the will of the Father
who is in heaven.   This is a lifetime job—it calls for no
vacations.   There is no superannuated chair to be occupied.   There is no time for retirement.   But ever hang-
ing like a banner in the air are the never-to-be-forgotten words of Paul the apostle, "Be instant in season, out
of season."   What is the answer to Paul's question when
he says, "How shall we escape, if we neglect so great salvation?"

Christ gives the answer.   When He talked to the
multitudes about His being the Bread of life and they
turned and walked away, He said to His own disciples,
"Will ye also go away?"   And Peter replied, "Lord, to
whom shall we go?   Thou hast the words of eternal life."
That's the answer—there is no escape.   But he who accepts the great salvation, when he comes to the end of
the journey, will say:

> O Captain!   My Captain!
>   Our fearful trip is done!
> The ship has weathered every wreck,

The prize we sought is won,
The port is near, the bells I hear,
The people all exulting.

The ship is anchored safe and sound;
Its voyage closed and done,
From fearful trip the victor ship
Comes in with object won.

Dr. and Mrs. Ayres of St. Louis, had compassion for the children who were homeless and began in a feeble way to provide a home in their city to house and feed a few little orphans. Thanksgiving Day was approaching and the little boys asked for turkey for Thanksgiving dinner. The good woman of the house informed them they were unable to purchase a turkey. That night, when the curtain of darkness had fallen, the little fellows held a prayer meeting in the alley and asked the Lord to send them a Thanksgiving turkey. Two or three mornings later, a turkey was moving about in the fenced yard around the home. No one seemed to know when it came or to whom it belonged. The turkey was found on the table for the Thanksgiving dinner.

A few days later, a man poorly dressed, knocked at the door, stating he was not well, was hungry and needed a home. Could the good lady of the house make room for him for a little while? She replied that to do so would work a great inconvenience and he walked away.

Soon after, Mrs. Ayres read in the morning paper the closing of a home in which seven old ladies had been cared for and that they had no place to go. She held consultation with her husband and they decided, although crowded, to make room for the old ladies in their own home. The news of their kindly act was published in one of the

St. Louis papers.   One morning thereafter the man who
had asked for shelter appeared at the door of the home,
shaven and well dressed, and said to Mrs. Ayres, "Before
Thanksgiving I was walking about and passed your
place. I heard the voices of little boys in a prayer meeting near your house. They were asking for a turkey. I
brought the turkey and placed it in your yard. Later, I
read of your having taken the seven homeless women into
your home. I am the man who came to your door and
asked if you could give me a home. You have been most
generous. I am a well-to-do bachelor with large sums of
money which I want to use while I live in helping some
one who knows how to use it in a benevolent way. Here
is my check." And to the surprise of the good woman, it
was a check for $92,000. That was in answer to prayer.
To the unbeliever it would seem simply as an incident, or
just one of those things that happen. To the Christian it
is the answer to prayer.

Helen Welshimer has written:

It was so dark along my little street—
    Day's end had come without a lighted lamp,
And I was lost as Israel's children were
    When they had toiled dim years in Egypt's camp.

I, too, it seemed, had made bricks all the day
    That other hands might build a monument;
My vessel held no oil to break the dusk
    Of alien fields where I had pitched my tent.

Then suddenly I prayed—and there was light
    That left me warm and strangely unafraid;
When I am frightened now I always think
    Once it was dark and light came when I prayed.

"PRAY AND DON'T FAINT"

Luke 18: 1

"Men ought always to pray, and not to faint." These are the words of Jesus, who believed in prayer. Prayer changes things. Prayer is power and it opens the avenue to untold blessings.

A sincere, praying people always will be a truly religious people. Christ is the finest example of a praying man. He was without sin, was the only begotten Son of God, was panoplied with power from God, was the only representative of perfect manhood, had miraculous power, and yet was a man of constant prayer.

Before the sunrise had tiptoed over the mountains in Galilee, as the curtains of the night were being drawn to admit the light of day, He was found in a place of prayer. He taught men to pray, and in the text today He said that men should pray and faint not. By that is meant in times of discouragement, sorrow, need, one is not to give up. To faint means to quit, to be overpowered. The teaching of Jesus is, use the blessing that is ready for you instead of giving up. Quitting is the last thing one should do. The world is full of quitters. The need in every avenue of life is for men to "stay put." Prayer is one of the aids.

Two hundred eighty-two times prayer is mentioned in the Bible. Jesus came up from the waters of baptism, praying. In Gethsemane, He took the three disciples of the inner circle farther from the gate and left them, while He went still farther, and there beneath the olive

16

trees prayed in such agony that He sweat great drops of blood. Once, He prayed for Peter, saying, "that thy faith fail not."

Prayer is not to be simply for great occasions, or only in the time of extreme need. We are admonished to "pray without ceasing." What is commonly known as "The Lord's Prayer," found in Matthew 6: 9-13, was a model prayer, the sample of the kind of prayer which the disciples were to use. Being impressed by the praying ability of John's disciples, His disciples came to Jesus, upon one occasion, and requested Him to teach them how to pray as John's disciples had been taught to pray. The prayer given here is simple and runs the whole gamut of man's desire. It is a brief prayer. All the prayers in the Scriptures are to the point, brief, and couched in plain language.

Let us study briefly this prayer. "After this manner therefore pray ye." He did not say to use these words, but pray in this manner. "Our Father which art in heaven." This is recognition of God, not merely as the Creator, the great cause of this physical universe, but He is more. He bears the relation of father to children. In that respect, God is love. Jesus said, "God so loved the world, that he gave his only begotten Son, that whosoever believeth in him should not perish, but have everlasting life." Addressing God as "Our Father" brings with it the recognition of Jesus the Christ as His Son.

The New Testament teaches that if one believes not in Jesus as the divine Son of God, then that individual is not a son of God. For, in speaking of Jesus, John says, "He came unto his own, and his own received him not. But as many as received him, to them gave he power to become the sons of God, even to them that believe on his name: which were born, not of blood, nor of the will of the flesh, nor of the will of man, but of God. And the Word was made flesh, and dwelt among us, (and we beheld his glory, the glory as of the only begotten of the Father,) full of grace and truth." God is the Father; Jesus is His only begotten Son, and we are adopted sons of God the Father. In Romans 8: 14-17, Paul said, "For as many as are led by the Spirit of God, they are the sons of God. For ye have not received the spirit of bondage again to fear; but ye have received the Spirit of adoption, whereby we cry, Abba, Father. The Spirit itself beareth witness with our spirit, that we are the children of God: and if children, then heirs; heirs of God, and joint-heirs with Christ; if so be that we suffer with him, that we may be also glorified together."

"Hallowed be thy name." This is having reverence for God, the highest respect. God is called "reverend" just once in all the Scriptures. Psalm 111: 9, referring to God, reads, "Holy and reverend is his name." It is entirely out of place for fallible men to assume that title of "reverend." That belongs to God and only to God. We reverence Him and not man.

"Thy kingdom come." That was the message of John the Baptist; also the Christ. It was not here in their day, but was in the offing. The kingdom and the church are synonymous. On the first Pentecost after the resurrection of the Christ, the Holy Spirit came, according to promise, and endued the apostolic group. And Peter, standing before the multitudes that day, spoke as the Spirit gave him utterance. That day the kingdom was ushered in to just as many as believed in

Christ. The kingdom is still coming as individuals accept Him. The thought is now that the kingdom be extended until the Christ is accepted and the knowledge of Him covers the earth as the waters cover the sea. The kingdom comes now to the unbeliever only as the gospel is preached, which is the incorruptible seed of the Word of God that begets men into a holy faith and leads them to obedience.

"Thy will be done on earth as it is in heaven." That means we pray that God's laws shall be obeyed, for His laws are the expression of His will.

"Give us this day our daily bread" is a prayer for food for each day. We live only in the present—day by day—for we have no promise of the morrow. Man and God work together for the daily bread. In the wilderness march from Egypt to Canaan, God furnished the manna which had in it all elements essential to building the body and maintaining life within that body. But men had to gather the manna and in the home bake it into bread. God makes all the provisions whereby bread can be given. He furnishes the germ of life in the seed. He blesses that seed with sun and rain and fertility of soil. But man must do the planting, the cultivating, the reaping and the preparation of that product for the table. Man and God work together always in the answer to prayer.

"Forgive us our debts." To trepass means to walk across, and when we walk across God's laws, we are trespassing. We are asking only that we be forgiven in the same spirit and in the same ratio with which we forgive those who trespass against us.

"Lead us not into temptation." The Scriptures teach

God tempts no man. The thought here is, may we not be led into temptation. We are told that if we resist the devil he will flee from us.

"Deliver us from evil." This is the prayer in which we depend upon God's strength and ask for His direction and that He will make it possible for us to be delivered from the evil one.

This is a comprehensive prayer. Nothing is omitted. There is nothing in it of selfishness.

The prayer which is in reality the Lord's own prayer is that found in John 17. There He prayed for Himself, for the apostles, for those who would hear their words and on down through the centuries for all who hear the gospel message. With foresight, looking through the corridors of time, and knowing the frailties of mankind, Jesus knew the dangers which would beset the people when they would be led to substitute for the plain Word of the Spirit the traditions of men. Christian unity was in the mind of the Christ and is stressed in that prayer.

Also, the apostle Paul saw it in his day and admonished the Corinthians that they should be united, have the same mind as was in Christ Jesus, all speak the same things, and that there should be no divisions among them. He referred to the church of that first century as being the body, that is, the organization of Christ, and he said there was just one body, one organization.

Unity should be prayed for and worked for today. The tragedy in the Christian ranks is the divisions, unauthorized by Christ, the Holy Spirit and the apostles; and as Christ prayed, so we should pray, that unity in doctrine, in polity and in life should prevail.

There are laws of prayer just as there are laws in the material world. Let us look at some of these.

1. We read that "the effectual fervent prayer of a righteous man availeth much." Prayer should not be halfhearted, cold, indifferent, half-believing, but must be in earnest.

2. "Pray without ceasing." This means consistent prayer, not merely on occasions. One can pray as one walks along the street, follows the plow, sits at a desk. Prayers do not need to be long. Peter's prayer, as he began to sink while walking on the sea was, "Lord, save, or I perish." The publican who prayed in the temple simply said, "Lord, be merciful unto me, a sinner." These men were not *saying* prayers; they prayed.

3. Christ admonished His disciples not to be like the Pharisees whom He denounced as hypocritical in prayer, for they loved to stand on street corners and pray aloud when folk were passing by. They prayed to be heard of men and their prayers did not ascend to God.

4. Christ places emphasis upon private prayers in the closet, or anywhere that affords secrecy, where a man can be alone and there meditate and pray. God hears him there. This is not condemnation nor a command against public prayers. But when one prays in public he should have the same spirit as one who prays in the closet and should not pray simply to show off, and to receive the compliments of men.

5. Use not vain repetitions, which means make the prayer simple. Do not repeat. Many people have a habit of addressing God as "Our heavenly Father" from ten to twenty times in prayer. That is vain repetition.

6. Prayer meetings are psychologically important and

are advocated by the Christ, for He said in Matthew 18:
19, 20: "Again I say unto you, That if two of you shall
agree on earth as touching any thing that they shall ask,
it shall be done for them of my Father which is in heav-
en. For where two or three are gathered together in my
name, there am I in the midst of them." In all prayers
one should remember that the Christ said, "Not my will,
but thine, be done," for God's will always is best. If we
observe the rules given by the Christ, we shall know how
to pray.

7. Pray for one another. Men need prayers in the
successful hours of life as well as in the tragic hours. A
young attorney won a very important case before the
courts while in a distant city, far removed from his
home. He wired his minister, "I won the case; pray
for me." He knew the danger of success.

Andrew Jackson heard his minister say one Sunday
morning that every Christian should pray in public. At
the next prayer meeting Jackson tried and made a mis-
erable muddle of it. His minister said to him that because it was such a great effort for him he would be re-
lieved from attempting to offer prayer in public here-
after. Jackson replied, "No, if that's the duty of a
Christian, I shall keep on." He did keep on, and the
day came when Andrew Jackson was the most gifted in
prayer of any within the congregation.

It is said that people in Brooklyn, New York, used
frequently to drop in to Henry Ward Beecher's service
for the opening worship just to hear him pray. Being
crowded for time, they then retired, but the prayer went
with them all the day. Prayer offered in sincerity and
in language easily understood has tremendous influence.

Some years ago in a great convention, one of the most eloquent ministers of the South was the preacher of the morning. Preceding the address, George Taubman, minister of First Christian Church in Long Beach, was called upon to offer the morning prayer. He prayed. He had a voice that wooed. He talked to God the Father as a child would speak to his earthly father. It was in the days of the First World War and hearts were tender. When Taubman closed that prayer, the entire audience was in tears. The meeting closed in a little while, and not a word was heard from any concerning the eloquence and oratory accompanying the message of the preacher, but everybody was moved and impressed by the prayer, and it was the topic of discussion. Yes, prayer changes things. Prayer helps to put the heart in tune with the Infinite. People in the sickroom, folk in trouble, all are brought nearer to God when somebody prays.

Ella Wheeler Wilcox said in her prayer:

> Let me this morning do something that shall take
>   A little sadness from the world's vast store,
> And may I be so favored as to make
>   Of joy's too scanty sum a little more.
> Let me not hurt, by any selfish deed
>   Or thoughtless word, the heart of foe or friend;
> Nor would I pass, unseeing, worthy need,
>   Or sin by silence when I should defend.
> However meager be my worldly wealth,
>   Let me give something that shall aid my kind—
> A word of courage, or a thought of health,
>   Dropped as I pass for troubled hearts to find.
> Let me tonight look back across the span
>   'Twixt dawn and dark, and to my conscience say—
> Because of some good act to beast or man—
>   "The world is better that I lived today."

"HAPPY MILLIONAIRES"

Luke 12: 15

"A man's life consisteth not in the abundance of the things which he possesseth."

Jesus was speaking to an innumerable multitude of people. The audience was so large that they trod one upon another. In the audience was a man who, like many another, brought his troubles with him to the service. He interrupted Jesus in the sermon by requesting that He speak to his brother that he divide the inheritance with him. Jesus stated that "a man's life consisteth not in the abundance of the things which he possesseth."

Here is a truth that is timely in all ages and among all people. Many a man in poor circumstances, who earns his bread by the sweat of his face, and others, likewise, in fairly good circumstances, look upon the man who has great riches with envy. To their way of thinking great possessions would be the end of all worry and care and would usher in for them halcyon days.

A group was sitting around the stove one winter's evening in the grocery store, talking about various things in an idle manner, when a Negro, a sort of worthless character in the community, said, "Ah wush ah had ten thousan' dollars." One of the boys replied, "And what would you do with ten thousand dollars?" The colored man replied, "Ah'd buy da' bes' houn' ah could fin', and a saddle hoss, and put da' res' ob da' money at interest, then spen' mah tahm huntin' coon and 'possum. Da' barkin' ob dat houn' would be music in mah ears. Ah'd feel lahk a millionahr." It takes more than that to make life, but many people look no higher than just that.

If the wishes of all the people would be granted, what a chaotic condition the world would be in. Laborers in the necessarily difficult tasks of life would be wanting. It would be about the laziest world one could imagine. Solomon had a wish granted. He asked the Lord to give him wisdom to go in and out before his people. That implied common sense to do the necessary things, to set a good example, to rule wisely and well, and to be a blessing to the people of his kingdom.

The happiest men in the world are not the millionaires. They have worries concerning which the great masses of humanity have no knowledge. It has well been said, "Uneasy lies the head that wears the crown." The same rule can be applied to the millionaires. They are troubled with demands for help from every quarter—the poor, the needy, the institutions of various kinds that need financial support, all besiege them. Today many of our millionaries are greatly troubled with labor problems. Strikes are seen on all sides. Taxes were never as high as at the present time.

R. A. Long, an outstanding Christian leader in Kansas City, was a millionaire. He made great gifts and was fairly besieged with requests which he could not grant. He lived in a beautiful house, had one of the finest farms in Missouri, written up one time in "The Country Gentleman" as the model farm. He had great possessions, was honored and respected everywhere. But he said that the happiest days of his life were back in the days of his younger manhood when he ran a little sawmill up in the great woods, and his wife and he stacked lumber at night. They slept the sleep of the just, they lived on humble fare, they had health, few troubles, and contentment. He said it was then that he was really a millionaire.

At the gate of the temple in Jerusalem, Peter and John were accosted by a lame man who never had walked—"lame from his mother's womb"—who was carried daily to the Gate Beautiful to ask alms of those who entered the temple. Peter said to him, "Silver and gold have I none, but such as I have give I unto thee." And instantly, taking the man's hand, the lame one was made whole. He ran, he leaped, he jumped for joy, and rushing into the temple he broke up the service with his praise. He had something worth more than millions. He was now a normal creature, walking like other people. He was a millionaire.

As I speak this morning, I am talking to a great audience of millionaires. But you have not rightly appraised your wealth. Health is worth millions to you. Many a person lying upon the bed of affliction, some grasping for life, some who never will leave that bed until carried to their tomb, would rather have health than all the gold of Old Cathay. This poem preaches a great sermon:

DON'T WHINE

"Today, upon a bus, I saw a lovely girl
    with golden hair,
Envied her, she seemed so gay, and wished
    I were as fair.
When suddenly she rose to leave, I saw her
    hobble down the aisle;
She had one leg, and wore a crutch; and as
    she passed—a smile.
O God forgive me when I whine.
I have two legs. The world is mine.

"And then I stopped to buy some sweets.
　　The lad who sold them had such charm
I talked with him—he seemed so glad—
　　if I were late 'twould do no harm.
And as I left he said to me: 'I thank you.
　　You have been so kind.
It's nice to talk with folks like you.'
　　'You see,' he said, 'I'm blind.'
　　O God forgive me when I whine.
　　I have two eyes. The world is mine.

"Later, walking down the street, I saw a
　　child with eyes of blue,
He stood and watched the others play;
　　it seemed he knew not what to do.
I stopped a moment, then I said: 'Why
　　don't you join the others, dear?'
He looked ahead without a word, and
　　then I knew—he could not hear.
　　O God forgive me when I whine.
　　I have two ears. The world is mine.

"With legs to take me where I'd go—
With eyes to see the sunset's glow—
With ears to hear what I would know—
　　O God forgive me when I whine.
　　I'm blessed indeed. The world is mine."

—Anonymous.

Do you have friends? If so, you're a millionaire.
Charles Lamb, who lived a beautiful life, had many troubles, but he looked on the bright side, counted his blessings and was cheerful. One asked him one day how he could be so contented. He replied, "I have a friend."
Lonely, indeed, and poor is he or she who has no friends.

Most of us think often of the home where we were born, for a while lived, labored, and loved. The church and the community in which we dwelt are sacred places in our thoughts. We love to go back to the scenes of our childhood. With the poet we can say, "Backward, turn backward, O time in your flight; make me a child again just for tonight." What is it that endears to you the place of your birth? The people that dwelt there! The association with folk — friends — that makes places dear! You are indeed a millionaire with the coming of the "patter of memories on the roof which the years have built above your head." One does not get far in this world without the help of friends.

He is a millionaire who has a happy home. When Jesus gave a picture of heaven He called it a home—the Father's house—and room for all. Of all the things of earth, there was none other with which He could so well describe heaven to citizens of the earth as by comparing it to a home. John Howard Payne who wrote, "Home, Sweet Home," was a tired, weary man who sat on the porch of a stranger's house as the curtains of the night were falling. He heard the prattle of little children and the song of a mother through the half-open door. He was impressed with the idea more than ever of the value and the joy of a home. He went to his dingy room and wrote the song that everybody loves — "Home, Sweet Home." In it he said, "Be it ever so humble, there's no place like home." He went away, and after awhile returned. His song had become quite famous. He went down the street and sat on the same porch in an evening hour and there heard a mother singing to her little brood, and it was his song. He is poor, indeed who is homeless; but he is rich, a millionaire, who has a good home. Grace Atkins describes a home as follows:

AFTER WORK

Little faces at the window,
　　Sparkling eyes with smiles as bright,
This is Daddy's royal welcome
　　When I come home at night.

A barricaded door!　It opens!
　　How the children laugh with glee
And the music of their laughter
　　Is like angel songs to me.

They rush to get my slippers,
　　They place them by my chair,
While they smother me with kisses
　　And tousel up my hair.

One hastens for the paper,
　　But who could read it now
While on my lap they frolic
　　Little hands upon my brow?

Little children's sweet caresses,
　　Little fingers in my hair,
When I count my many riches
　　I'm a multimillionaire!

And Ida Josephine Brittain has described it thus:

A HOME

A home is not a house—
　　A home is several things!
It is a kitchen stove
　　On which a kettle sings;

It is a table set
　　With care and loving thought,
Where conversation's cheer
　　And fellowship are wrought;

> It is a well-worn chair
>   Beneath a shaded light;
> Or perhaps a cherished book
>   By a log fire at night;
>
> It is a quiet place
>   For prayer, or for rest,
> Or just to be alone
>   When aloneness is best.
>
> A home is not a house,
>   But it is a several things
> Within high walls of love
>   Where contentment clings.

You can not buy a home; you buy a house, and you make a home.

A man is a millionaire who has a good conscience—a conscience free of offense to God and man. He is happiest who can rise in the morning, and looking into the heavens say to God, "It's all right between you and me," and then looking about him, say to his fellow men, "It's all right between you and me." No load is so heavy to carry as the load of a bad conscience. The man with a bad conscience is like the boy who paid no attention to the advice of his father and mother, went into the far country, forgot home training, church, and Christian friends. He spent his substance in riotous living. He committed a crime which placed him behind prison bars, and through the night he could be heard saying, "If I only had, if I only had," meaning if he had only given ear and heart to the teaching of his parents. A good conscience is the best tonic and the best support to any one in life's struggle.

He is a millionaire who has work. God ordained that

a man should earn his living by the sweat of his brow, and also decreed that a man should work six days, one day being taken for rest and for worship. Many a man who toils envies the millionaire whose hands are not hard and horny from toil, whose clothing is without spot or wrinkle, but whose brain may be in a whirling storm. A minister in Canton in the early days of my ministry said to me one day, "When I see men passing my home in the early morning and returning in the evening with their lunch baskets, going home for a good night's sleep, no worries about the many things with which I am concerned, I feel I would like to exchange places." On the other hand, the laboring man ofttimes wishes he had an easier role to play in life. Helen Welshimer puts it in these words in her poem,

A SONG OF TOIL

America is working! Once again
　　There is the sound of labor in the land.
Flame-bright the forges light the ending dark,
　　And tasks begin for every reaching hand.
There is the ring of anvils in the night,
　　The swing of axes, march of workers' feet,
And steel flows molten, shining as a dream—
　　Now we have learned shrill whistles may be sweet!

Triumphantly the flag waves high and free
　　Above the smoke where industry begins,
Above the busyness of shops and stores,
　　Above the hearts purged clean of idle sins.
Oh, always it is good to have a task,
　　The plan of life must grant some work to men.
So let the bugles play, the deep drums throb,
　　America has gone to work again!

If you have health, a home, work to do, a good conscience, and friends, and you live in the United States,
you should be a happy millionaire. In what other country could you live where you have the liberties which you
enjoy in the United States? Every man is a king and
every woman a queen, in this country. We can worship
God according to the dictates of our own conscience, we
have free speech, freedom of press, a great educational
system, harvests unsurpassed anywhere else in the world.
Millions living in servitude in many countries are de-
prived of the real necessities of life. The children never
know what it is to have their hunger satisfied and go to
bed on a full stomach. A great poet, when he had
traveled about the world and had seen all the wealth, as
well as the poverty and the distress, said:

> So it's home again, and home again
>   America for me!
> I want a ship that's westward bound
>   Across the rolling sea
> To the blessed land of "room enough"
>   Beyond the ocean bars,
> Where the air is full of sunlight, and
>   The flag is full of stars.

A millionaire? He is the happiest and the greatest
one who has become an heir of God and joint heir with
Jesus Christ, who has the promise of immortality and
knows that when the silver cord loosens and the golden
bowl breaks and the curtain falls on the stage where he
has played his part, he will enter into the "land of pure
delight." Paul saw the treasures over there in his vision
one night, and said that ever after that vision he had a desire to be "absent from the body and to be present with

the Lord." And when that hour came, from his dungeon in Rome he wrote to Timothy and said, "I am now ready to be offered. The time of my departure is at hand. I have fought a good fight, I have finished my course, I have kept the faith; henceforth there is laid up for me a crown of righteousness, which the Lord, the righteous judge, shall give me at that day; and not to me only, but unto all them that love his appearing." And when the axman lifted the ax and the head of him who belonged to the grand army of the redeemed rolled lifeless in the dust, his spirit mounted into the presence of the King.

Jesus said, "What shall it profit a man if he gain the whole world and lose his own soul?" The rich man whom Jesus described, who wore purple and fine linen and fared sumptuously every day, was a millionaire here, while the poor boy that lay at his gate, hungry for the crumbs which fell from the rich man's table, was a pauper here. But the scene shifts. The rich man was carried by some of his friends to his grave. Lazarus, the beggar, was carried to the heavenly home by the angels. Here the rich man was a millionaire; there, he was a pauper. Lazarus was a pauper here, but there he was a millionaire.

Life is more than possessing things, be they few or many. And every man is very largely the architect of his own fortune or misfortune.

"THE GLOW AND THE GLOOM OF THE MINISTRY"

Philippians 1: 18

"Christ is preached; and I therein do rejoice."—Philippians 1: 18. "O that I had wings like a dove, for then would I fly away and be at rest."—Psalm 55: 6.

Here are two statements concerning life. Paul the apostle, who is not ashamed of the gospel of Christ, said, "I labored more abundantly than they all," and he represents one who saw the glow of the ministry. The other saw the gloomy side of service. These represent the ups and downs of those who serve. Elijah, the prophet, after the victory on Mount Carmel, was disappointed in his reception as he stood at the gates of Jezreel, where the wicked Jezebel threatened his life. He fled for three days into the wilderness and lay down beneath the juniper tree and prayed the Lord to take away his life, for he had not been as good, as successful as were his fathers. Elijah was stressing the gloomy side.

Jeremiah, the prophet in Jerusalem, sometimes called "the weeping prophet," for his task was a difficult one, was misunderstood, much abused, and in one of his despondent moments said, "O that I had in the wilderness a lodging place of wayfaring men; that I might leave my people and go from them! They are adulterers and treacherous men." Here again the prophet saw the gloomy side. In the discussion to follow, let us present the gloomy side first.

There is no higher calling than that of the Christian

ministry. James A. Garfield, who did some preaching while president of Hiram College, was visited one day by a preacher friend, after Mr. Garfield had become President of the United States. The friend had made no great place for himself in the ministry, felt that his services were not fully appreciated and came to ask the President to place him in a government position in which his salary would be above that paid him in the ministry. He felt he could be of more service in the government than in the pulpit. President Garfield told him he had no position to offer him which would be superior to that of the ministry. He advised him to return to his pastorate and to seek the glow that is to be found in the preaching of the gospel.

The responsibility of having the gospel proclaimed to all the world has been laid upon the hearts of Christian men and women. In the Great Commission Jesus stated the plan before His valedictory and His ascension beyond all the heavens to be with God the Father. Jesus had made no other arrangements. Not to angels, but to men was the charge given to go into all the world and preach the gospel to every creature.

The apostles, the chosen, prepared ambassadors of our Lord, did not rest on flowery beds of ease. They knew the meaning of sacrifice and suffering. They were misunderstood, mistreated, and unappreciated. They suffered martyrdom, banishment, but they faltered not, stayed put, and triumphed over every obstacle. Like their Master they met the gloom and refused not the glow until the hour of their departure.

The church, the body or organization of Christ on this earth, has a twofold task. It is to call and to help prepare young men and women for the Christian service in the ministry of the Word, or in some other phase of kingdom building. The church is commanded to look to the fields already white unto the harvest and to pray to the Lord to send forth laborers into His harvest. The church must discover and persuade the right type of individuals to prepare for this, the greatest of all work.

It is also the duty of the church, and should be its pleasure upon receiving one of these servants to be its minister, to help develop the preacher of the Word that he may grow and glow in his ministry.

A young man has not learned it all when he walks from college and seminary with his diploma. Much remains to be learned. Commencement Day exercises were closing. A young lady emerged from the hall, stood on the steps and viewed the world as it stood upon the campus. Waving her diploma she said, "Good morning, World, I have my A. B." And the World replied, "Come on, young lady, and we'll teach you the rest of the alphabet." So it is when a young preacher enters upon his ministry—he has to learn the rest of the alphabet. And the church he serves must help him.

Years ago a young preacher from Kentucky was called to preach a sermon in a small church located in a new section of Kansas City. The youthful preacher preached his sermon, following which an elder said, "Brother Combs, you come to Independence Boulevard, remain with us, and we'll make of you a great preacher." He went, he stayed and he became an outstanding pulpiteer.

The church has the making or the breaking of the preacher. He will have days of gloom and there will be days of the glow.

E. B. Wakefield, one of God's saints having a profes-
sor's chair in Hiram College, had been a successful minister in the Christian Church in Warren, Ohio. He knew
all the ups and downs, the glow and the gloom of the
ministry. One day he said to the class which was about
to graduate, "Young men, there will be times in your
ministry when you will come home from the service and
feel like bumping your head against the wall and selling
out to the devil for a dollar." He spoke wisely and truth-
fully. Where is there a minister who sometime has not
felt just that way?

In my first year in the ministry in Canton a brilliant
young man just out of high school, reporting on one of
Canton's daily papers, came to interview me. He said,
"I have been considering whether or not to enter the ministry." And he added, "I have been offered a scholar-
ship in a large seminary if I will enter the ministry of
that church." I said to him, "What is your purpose in
entering the ministry?" And to this he replied, "It affords an easy life, gives plenty of time to read, to study
and to think, and one is associated with good people."
The young man had no idea of Christian service. He
saw not the gloom, the arduous work, the sacrificial spirit
and discerned not the sympathetic word and touch so essential to the successful ministry. All he saw was the
glow which would come from blessings he himself, as he
thought, would receive. Thank God, he did not enter
the ministry! The pulpit and the pastorate have no place
for such as he.

Coming on down to our day, what is the gloom which
the minister of the Word sometimes will face? Lack of
co-operation on the part of the church membership causes

many a man to spend sleepless nights, to be bowed down
with grief and to feel with Jeremiah that he longs for a
lodging place in the wilderness.

The minister is a leader. He lives with the work of
the church, while many of his members are busily em-
ployed in other vocations. He must think and plan and
inspire the co-operation, support, and fellowship of the
flock over which he is shepherd. One parishoner, when
asked by another one day why he did not accept a responsibility that had been assigned him replied, "We pay the
preacher for doing that; let him do it." The preacher
has more to do than simply attempting to keep people
sweet, ringing door bells, wear out shoe soles, settling all
troubles and misunderstandings that come up in the
church, and to be a general all-around errand boy. He
does the best work who has the ability to create desire on
the part of the membership to be "workers together with
God." He does well who can assign duties, keep all of
his people happy in the service they render. That, too,
makes for a church of peace.

A farmer had a team of mules. He said of them,
"They can outpull anything in our neighborhood. They
can take the blue ribbon when it comes to kicking, too.
But they never pull and kick at the same time." What
is true of mules is true of folk. Keep them busy, and
they haven't time to kick.

Empty pews give the preacher gloom. Those pews
have no ears to hear. There is no inspiration in preaching to wood. Nothing is so discouraging to a preacher
as to prepare his message for a people who need that message, then to look out over the audience assembled and
find that two-thirds of his membership is not present.

Then he begins to worry, has sleepless nights. Are they offended at something he has said or done, has he been neglectful of duty, are the people tired of his message, has he not preached a full gospel, are his people strolling into some other church, have they had a quarrel with some individual in the church—what is the trouble? He spends the night in wonderment and worry and the following day in beating pathways to the homes of some to ascertain why the absence.

Bert Wilson, Christian minister, a few years ago sent out a questionnaire to many churches of different denominations, asking what percentage of the church membership was regular in attendance. A cross section revealed that an average of about 33% of the membership of any church was regular in attendance. When one came to church, there were two others who ought to have been there and who remained at home.

A strong denominational church in Ohio with a magnificent building, a good man in the pulpit, with an assistant minister known as the pastor, with a lady church visitor, and two office secretaries, plus an educational director has a membership of 2,500. For four weeks that group kept a record of the membership in attendance at the Sunday morning service, the only preaching service of the day. And out of that 2,500 membership, there was never as many of 500 in the audience on any Lord's Day morning of the month. Do you wonder that the minister of the church experienced the gloom?

It is a gloomy day for the preacher when his church membership consecrates its talents, its time, its influence, and its money to business only, or to the group or social life of the community and neglects the church, the divine institution, the body of the Christ, the only agency which stands pre-eminently for the salvation of man. It is fine when a church member lets his light shine and is active in the organizations of his community that are altruistic, but never should he think of abandoning his church any more than a mother would abandon her children to help other families. Here is a family who has been zealous in the church, gradually becomes cold, slackens up its attendance and finally drifts away and comes no more — backsliders. These are the sins that cause a preacher to experience the gloom which shakes him like the ague.

In times like this the preacher should be comforted by the words of the poet:

> "Be still sad heart and cease repining,
> Behind the clouds the sun is still shining;
> Thy fate is the common fate of all,
> Into each life some rain must fall,
> Some days must be dark and dreary."

There is another side to the ministry and that's the glow. When a preacher is in health, has time to prepare his sermons, knows the needs of his people and on the Lord's Day faces his well-filled house and proclaims the glorious gospel to waiting, listening, appreciative ears, he experiences the glow of the ministry.

When the invitation is extended and people come down the aisles to accept Jesus the Christ, the preacher has the glow that no other knows. When in his church he sees little tots from the Cradle Roll up through the elementary departments and on up to the young people being trained, he looks upon the church of tomorrow and feels that his labors are not in vain.

When the preacher is the shepherd of the flock and the sheep hear his voice and appreciate his service, he feels the glow of the ministry. To be with the people in the times of sunshine and shadow, when skies are clear and when they are dark, in the hour of sickness and the sorrowing hour of death, just to be able to render the service that removes the sting and sorrow from tears that flow, he has experienced the glow of the Christian ministry.

When his people come to him for counsel and conference, when he is able to help them, and when the curtains of the night fall about him and the tasks of the day have been completed, just to look back and to note how many times he has really been helpful to some soul, that manifests the glow of the ministry.

To be instrumental in helping people to be better, happier, and more useful is a joy to the life of any good man or woman. Some one has said: "He is a benefactor who makes two blades of grass grow where formerly only one was growing." Likewise, he is a benefactor who can drive away the gloom, dry the tear and bring a smile to a troubled heart. There is no other life which can surpass that of the minister in "going about doing good." The greatest preacher of all time did just that. He knew the glow of service and He experienced the gloom, but He never gave up, but steadfastly moved on.

Our day demands a strong voice to quiet the storm that rages in the minds of multitudes of people. Wars, cold and hot, many thousands of our youth being led to the slaughter, uncertainty prevailing everywhere! The weary old world is looking for rest and for peace, and prays that the purple testament of war may be closed forever. In this day a glow comes to the preacher's life when he can preach the Word, give assurance and quiet the storms that rage in many a breast, as did the Galilean preacher who spoke to the angry winds and the waves, "Peace be still."

Goldsmith in "The Deserted Village" pictures the glow of the village preacher in the following words:

"His best companions, innocence and health; and his best riches, innocence and wealth."

"While resignation gently slopes the sea and all his purposes binding to the last; his heaven commences e'er the world be passed."

"A man he was to all the country dear, and passing rich with forty pounds a year."

"Careless their merits or their faults to scan,
His pity gave ere charity began.
Thus to relieve the wretched was his pride,
And even his failings lean'd to Virtue's side.

"And as a bird each fond, endearment tries
To tempt its new-fledg'd offspring to the skies,
He tried each art, reprov'd each dull delay,
Allur'd to brighter worlds, and led the way.
"Even children follow'd with endearing wile,
And pluck'd his gown, to share the good man's smile.

"As some tall cliff, that lifts its awful form,
Swells from the vale, and midway leaves the storm,
Though 'round its breast the rolling clouds are spread,
Eternal sunshine settles on its head."

So it is with the preacher who enjoys the glow of the ministry.

"WORDS--WORDS--WORDS"

Psalm 119: 130

"The entrance of thy word giveth light." Shakespeare said, "Words, words, words." We make a like remark when all we do is talk but are slow to act. Nevertheless, words are power; they have their place. A word is the expression of an idea. By words we make known our desires. They are the means of communication among individuals.

It is written, "As a man thinketh in his heart, so is he." As he speaks he reveals his thoughts. As Peter warmed himself by the enemy's fire on the night of Jesus' trial, a girl said to him, "Thy speech betrayeth thee." She had reference to his dialect. His words showed the country from which he came. The spoken word frequently, likewise, betrays us and tells how we think, how we feel and gives expression to our attitudes.

Words convey God's will to man. The angel of the Lord told Cornelius in Caesarea to send to Joppa for Peter, the preacher, saying, "He will tell you words whereby you can be saved."

When the enemies of Jesus had tried all known means to entrap Him and all had failed, their last move was to get Him to talk. Many a man has given himself away when he talked too much. It is the attorney's delight to get the witness on the stand to talk overmuch, as thereby he is more easily caught in the trap. What a blessing speech is to humanity! It is a lonely old world for any man or woman who can not speak.

It is written in the Proverbs, "A good word maketh the heart glad." A poor, but fairly well-dressed man, penniless, stood one evening in a restaurant looking at the food which adorned the cafeteria counters. He was homeless, lonely, and hungry. A young man came hurriedly in for some change and said to the stranger, "My good friend, can you change a five-dollar bill for me?" And the stranger replied, "I haven't a penny to my name, but I thank you, dear fellow, for calling me 'friend.'"

"A word spoken in due season, how good it is!" There are seasons in one's life when the right word is greatly needed. In the season of sickness a cheery word, a prayer welling up from the heart, expressing itself in words, bring comfort and strength many times to those on whom sickness has laid its hand. The same is true in the case of death. The entrance of an old friend, the word of sympathy gently spoken, the proof given that the sorrowing one is not forgotten, bring gladness to the heart of the one who mourns. "A good word maketh the heart glad."

The appreciative word is much desired. Edgar De-Witt Jones, of Detroit, preached one Sunday to a large audience in the Calvary Baptist Church of the capital city. His subject was, "We Would See Jesus." The writer sat where he had a good view of Supreme Court Justice Charles Evans Hughes, who listened intently to the sermon. Dr. Jones told me later that on Monday morning a letter was delivered to him from Chief Justice Hughes, who wrote to thank him for the sermon which he had heard the day before. Needless to say, that letter is preserved in the files of the preacher.

A teacher in the Canton public schools, who was the teacher of the writer's two daughters, at the time they were in grade school, was retiring. We wrote her a letter commending her for her good work and thanking her for the fine service rendered to our daughters and to hundreds of others. She replied to that letter that in the long years of her arduous service that was the only letter she ever had received from any parent, giving her thanks for services rendered. There are many individuals who go through life performing their duties and deeds unheralded, who are hungry for a word of appreciation. The due season is here for most people every day, and we fail to speak the word that would help to roll away the stone and set their spirits free. People need that word when death comes to their fireside and calls away a loved one. In the hours of adversity, at the period of lonesomeness, in the tragedies of life, how good it is for the right word to be spoken. It is written, "A word fitly spoken is like apples of gold in pictures of silver."

"A soft word turneth away wrath . . . grievous words stirreth up anger." Soft words are not silly words, but they are words that help.

In a county-seat town in Ohio a half century ago, the superintendent of the public schools was under the necessity of inflicting punishment upon a belligerent student, who was the son of a German butcher. The boy went home and told his story. The next morning, with murder in his eyes and cursing upon his lips, the big burly man from the meat market came rushing into the corridor of the school building, mounted the stairs and entered the office of the superintendent. At his right stood the son who yesterday had been punished. The superintendent was a wise man. He knew human nature and the power of words. Instead of flying into a rage, he kept his poise and pleasantly greeted his guest. The father was permitted to say only this: "I have come to see about my boy." From there on the conversation was one-sided. The superintendent kindly enumerated many of the fine qualities of the boy. Then bringing the lad into his office he told the father of the things the boy had been doing and for which he had received punishment. Up to this moment the father had said nothing, but his mind had been made up on the way to the schoolhouse as to what he was going to do. Having spoken kindly with much feeling and interest in the boy's welfare, the superintendent captivated the mind of the father and when he turned to leave the office, the father simply said, "Please, Mr. Superintendent, may I have a few words?" He thanked the superintendent for his interest in the boy, and the tempest that was raging in his heart when he came was gone. He had had time to listen to reason and soft words; the words fitly spoken had touched his heart and he turned as he left the office and said "I thank you. I feel my boy is safe in your hands. If again he disobeys your words, punish him more severely than you did yesterday." With these words he left. He had been won by "words fitly spoken." The soft words to which he had listened had turned away his wrath, whereas had the words been grievous, they would have stirred up his anger.

Daniel Webster, on his first day at college, stood a lonely, homesick boy, on the steps. Rufus King passed him and sensing his feelings, laid his hand on Daniel's shoulder and said, "Daniel, I know your father. Study hard and you are bound to succeed." In after years when the voice of Webster was rocking the United States Senate, he said from the floor of that body one day, "I still can feel the pressure of the hand of Rufus King on my shoulder. He spoke to me in that hour when a battle was raging within my soul.

Kind words never die. Longfellow said:

> "I shot an arrow into the air,
> It fell to earth, I knew not where;
> For, so swiftly it flew, the sight
> Could not follow it in its flight.
>
> I breathed a song into the air,
> It fell to earth, I knew not where
> For who has sight so keen and strong
> That it can follow the flight of song?
>
> Long, long afterwards, in an oak
> I found the arrow, still unbroke;
> And the song, from beginning to end,
> I found again in the heart of a friend."

Encouraging words pay great dividends. A prominent eye physician and surgeon in Canton, one of four sons and a daughter of a widowed mother, after graduation from high school went to work in one of Canton's largest factories. The president of the company passed his machine one day and calling him by name said, "What is your purpose in life?" The young man replied, "I would like to be a physician." The president simply said, "Don't say 'I'd like to be,' say, 'I'm going to be,' " and passed on to another machine. The words made their impression. They came like the ringing of the bells at dawn, day after day in the mind of that boy. He went to college, graduated, went to medical school and graduated, and today he is one of Canton's most prominent eye physicians and surgeons. "A word fitly spoken" in season was all that was needed.

Years ago, Myron T. Herrick, having graduated from college, came home to teach a rural school in northern Ohio. One day the school door opened and a tramp stepped in, went to the blackboard and wrote: "Whatsoever thy hand findeth to do, do it with thy might." He turned, walked out and away. The teacher told the boys to take that as the copy to be written that day in their copybooks in penmanship. They did so. The next morning when school opened one of the boys was not present. He had disappeared as suddenly as if the earth had swallowed him up. Years went by, but Dick never returned. Myron T. Herrick was later elected to the governorship of Ohio. His secretary one day entered his office with the announcement that a stranger was in the outer office and desired to see him. Governor Herrick said, "Usher him in." The man entered, and the governor recognized him at once with the words, "Dick, where have you been all these years?" Then Dick told his story. He had gone to South America. He prospered in the things to which he had applied his hands and he had become wealthy. He built and endowed a school in the South. After telling the story, he carefully took from his pocket the sheet on which the motto of the tramp had been recorded, and said, "Governor, do you remember that day the tramp wrote these words on the blackboard of our rural school? I kept that sheet, and those words have been my guiding star. I have come today to make a report and to thank you personally for having imprinted within my mind that great sentence, 'whatsoever thy hand findeth to do, do it with thy might.'"

To Timothy, Paul wrote, "Be thou an example to un-believers in word and conversation," which simply means, "Be a gentleman at all times, in all places; and speak the words that are helpful." The power of a thought ex-pressed is well told by Ella Wheeler Wilcox:

"I gave a beggar from my little store of wealth, some gold;
 He spent the shining ore and came again, and yet again,
Still cold and hungry as before.
I gave a thought, and through that thought of mine he found him-self,
The man supreme, divine;
Fed, clothed, and crowned with blessings manifest.
And now he begs no more."

The poet has said:

"If I sing a song when skies are gray,
 To help me face another day,
 Who knows but the echo
 May reach and strengthen
 The heart of another,
 When shadows lengthen.

"If I breath a prayer and it wings its way
 To the throne of God at close of day,
 Who knows but in passing it leaves behind
 A thread of faith that another may find."

God speaks to us in words recorded in the sacred vol-ume. The prophet Isaiah said, "The word of God shall stand for ever." God also said "My word shall not return to me void."

Many of the troubles to be found in business and social circles and in the homes are due to words unwisely spo-ken, or the lack of words being spoken at all. One has said:

"Five things in life observe with care:
  To whom you speak, of whom you speak,
  How, when, and where."

"We have kindly thought for the stranger,
    And smiles for the transient guest;
  But oft for our own there's the bitter tone,
    Though we love our own the best."

Yes—*Words*—*Words*—*Words*—a power for good—
or for evil.

"A PROPHET...LIKE UNTO MOSES"

Deuteronomy 18:15

"The Lord thy God will raise up unto thee a Prophet from the midst of thee, of thy brethren, like unto me; unto him ye shall hearken."

Moses was addressing the people of Israel. He was pointing them to the Christ who would be "the Prophet like unto himself." The bondage of the people of Israel, their deliverance from that bondage with Moses as the leader, their passing from Egypt into the wilderness on the dry land through the sea—all the incidents connected with the wilderness march and the final crossing of the Jordan into the promised land is a type of the deliverance of the man of the world from sin. In First Corinthians 10:1-11 Paul refers to all these events as a type and says, "Now all these things happened unto them for ensamples: and they are written for our admonition, upon whom the ends of the world are come."

In the sermon of today it is our purpose to show how Moses was a type of Christ—"a prophet like unto Moses." Their lives were very much alike in many respects. God commanded Moses to inform the people that in coming time there would be a Prophet from among their own folk who would speak for Jehovah, and unto Him the people were to give heed. It is interesting in studying the life of both Moses and the Christ to note in what ways they were much alike. This difference is to be noted —Moses was altogether human; while Jesus was the only begotten Son of God and was divine. Moses was imper-

51

fect in many ways; Jesus was the perfect man. In this sermon we are concerned only with the points of similarity.

1. Note the circumstances connected with their birth. When Moses was born an edict had gone forth demanding the extermination of male children of the Israelites. The king of Egypt spoke to the Hebrew midwives and said, "When ye do the office of a midwife to the Hebrew women, if it be a son, then ye shall kill him, but if it be a daughter, then she shall live" (Exodus 1: 15, 16). The midwives feared God and gave no heed to the king's demands. The command then went forth that when sons were born they should be cast into the river. In the meantime, Moses was born. When he was three months old and he could no longer be hid, the mother made a little ark of bulrushes, daubed it with slime and pitch, laid the baby in it, and he was hid in the flags by the river's brink. Little sister, Miriam, watched that ark as it rested there. The daughter of the Pharaoh, coming to wash herself, saw the ark, and when it was opened she saw the little, weeping baby. Miriam offered to find a nurse for the child. The offer was accepted and she brought the mother of the babe, who took the child and nursed him until the time when he no longer could be hid in the home, but had to be taken to the Pharaoh's daughter. He was reared in luxury and educated in the university of Egypt. And they named him Moses, meaning "drawn from the water."

When Jesus was born, Herod was disturbed and ordered the male children under two years of age to be slain in order that the one who was to be the king might be put to death. And to be sure that the right one was slain, all were ordered to be killed. Joseph and Mary, being warned of this danger, were commanded to take the child into Egypt, which they did, and there remained until the death of Herod. Then they returned to Nazareth, where Jesus grew to manhood, was subject unto His parents, and was in favor with God and man. In both cases, these babes were saved by the protecting hand of God.

2. Both lost a position of high estate and came to the service of mankind. Moses resided in the palace of Pharaoh, and possessed all the honor, riches, luxuries that Egypt could afford. When he came to mature years he left those surroundings, humbled himself, and through a force of circumstances went into the wilderness, where for forty years he was unknown, lived a simple, humble life, herding the flocks and herds, until, at the age of eighty, God called him to be the emancipator of his people, and their leader from bondage to liberty.

Jesus, likewise, was with God at the time of creation. He had glory with Him. He was the Prince of heaven, but He condescended to take on the nature of man and met the conditions which men have to meet. He was born of humble people. Mary, the mother, was a girl of character, but human. Her husband, Joseph, was simply known as the legal father of Jesus. But He who was with God in creation was the only begotten Son of God. And though, when with the Father He was rich, for our sakes He became poor. Here He was a ministering servant. In these facts He was "the Prophet like unto Moses."

3. Moses was the selected deliverer of his people. They were oppressed, held as slaves, and were subject unto Pharaoh. They cried for deliverance from burdens that were unbearable. Moses, the man who had learned the ways of the wilderness, was selected of God to be the

recipient of great powers, and to take the position of leader, to bring his people out of bondage.

Jesus came finding the world in the bondage of sin. He was sent to lead men out of bondage into liberty, from sin into righteousness. At the age of thirty He received the anointing of the Holy Spirit at the time of His baptism, began His ministry in Capernaum, and for little more than three years "went about doing good." To the aching hearts of the world He said, "Come unto me, all ye that labour and are heavy laden, and I will give you rest."

Peter introduced Him in his Pentecostal sermon by saying, "Ye men of Israel, hear these words: Jesus of Nazareth, a man approved of God among you by miracles and wonders and signs, which God did by him in the midst of you, as ye yourselves also know."

4. Both were lawgivers. Moses gave the law to Israel when he received it from God on Mt. Sinai. It is known as the law of Moses. The giving of that law marked the birth of the Jewish nation. It remained in force until the birth of the church, the beginning of the new covenant, and of the Christian dispensation on that first Pentecost after Jesus has ascended unto the Father. Jesus, not Moses, is our lawgiver. He has given us a perfect code of laws. Before He ascended He said, "All power is given unto me in heaven and in earth. Go ye therefore, and teach all nations, baptizing them in the name of the Father, and of the Son, and of the Holy Spirit, teaching them to observe all things whatsoever I have commanded you: and, lo, I am with you alway, even unto the end of the world." So as Moses stood at the head of the old dispensation, Jesus is at the head of the Christian

dispensation. Moses led the people through the wilderness to the Jordan, ready for deliverance into Canaan. Jesus leads the Christian in the wilderness of this earthly life until he comes to the Jordan of death, and then He leads on across that river into the heavenly Canaan.

5. Angels attended the ministration of both. In Acts 7: 53, Stephen, in his defense, told his murderers that they had received the law by the disposition of angels and had not kept it. When the law was given, God spoke through Moses, saying, "I send an Angel before thee, to keep thee in the way, and to bring thee unto the place which I have prepared." The life of Jesus was associated with the ministry of angels. They announced His coming, proclaimed His birth, were with Him in the wilderness, were present at the transfiguration, gave Him support in the garden of suffering, were present at His sepulcher, and attended Him as He ascended into glory.

6. Moses and Jesus stand at the head of the list of the best men the world ever has produced. Moses was God's mouthpiece to men. He was obedient in all the commands given him and is said to have been the meekest of men. He fasted and prayed and continually communed with God. Jesus, likewise, was obedient to every command of His heavenly Father. In Him there was no sin. He was the one perfect man. He was meek and lowly and gentle. It is said, "He strove not, neither did he cry, or lift up his voice in the street." He practiced self-denial, prayed without ceasing, and spent forty days and nights in the wilderness, fasting. When he was transfigured His countenance shone like the sun and His garments were glittering like the lightning. Twice God spoke and called Him "beloved Son."

7. Both were prophets. A prophet is one who speaks for another. Moses was the mouthpiece of God; Jesus spoke for the Father. The prophecies given by each came true. They could not have spoken of the things of which they did speak had they not been inspired of God. Moses had no other way of knowing about the things concerning which he prophesied except as the knowledge was given him from God. He was the prophet of the most High. Jesus likewise said that He spoke the mind of God. He never went to school. He was reared in a town from which no great men ever had come. Yet, the "common people heard him gladly." And those who were His enemies said, "Never a man so spake." He was the world's only extemporaneous speaker. In the real sense, there have been no others. Not one of His utterances has been improved upon. No sentence that fell from His lips has been or can be revised. He owed none of this to any school of earth. The answer is the Father was with Him.

8. Both men served the people. Moses for forty years led Israel. When they were thirsty he smote the rock and gave them drink; when hungry, manna from heaven came. When there were plagues he commanded them to look to the brazen serpent and be healed. All of his interest centered in their welfare in the wilderness journey. Jesus, likewise, "went about doing good." He healed the sick, fed the hungry, comforted the sorrowing, and was the friend of all mankind.

9. Both were misunderstood and treated with ingratitude. Israel rebelled frequently against Moses. They one time picked up stones to stone him. They mourned because they had left Egypt and longed for the food of

the land of their bondage. At times they suggested turning back and would gladly have rejected his authority. Jesus was not happily received, for "he came unto his own, and his own received him not; but as many as received him, to them gave he the power to become the sons of God." The enemies of Jesus crucified Him, but His spirit returned from paradise to reoccupy His body, and He arose on the third day, and triumphed over His enemies.

10. The people of Israel we are told were baptized into Moses in the cloud and in the sea. And in that he was their leader. The believer in Christ is baptized into the Christ. Paul states, "As many of you as were baptized into Christ did put on Christ." Moses, the leader, brought his people to the end of the wilderness life, ready to cross the Jordan into the promised land. Jesus, our leader, leads on until we come to the Jordan of death. Having followed our leader, we cross that little strip of sea—death—which separates this life from that beyond, for evermore to be with the Lord. But Paul tells us in the Hebrew epistle we "ought to give the more earnest heed to the things which we have heard, lest at any time we should let them slip. For if the word spoken by angels was stedfast, and every transgression and disobedience received a just recompense of reward; how shall we escape, if we neglect so great salvation; which at the first began to be spoken by the Lord, and was confirmed unto us by them that heard him."

"THE CONVERSION OF THE ETHIOPIAN"

Acts 8: 35

"Then Philip opened his mouth and began at the same scripture and preached unto him Jesus."

The Acts of the Apostles is the authentic book on the Christian evangelism of the apostolic age. Men guided by the Holy Spirit did the preaching. The message delivered in all places was in full agreement with the terms of salvation stipulated in the Great Commission.

The incidents in the story in the eighth chapter of the Acts were in that period when Saul was persecuting the Christians. The disciples retreated from Jerusalem and were scattered abroad, going everywhere preaching the Word. Philip was a deacon in the church at Jerusalem. He went down to the city of Samaria and preached Christ. Great results followed his preaching. He was given miraculous power and his miracles attracted the people, but his sermons won them to Christ. It is said "the people with one accord gave heed unto those things which Philip spake, hearing and seeing the miracles which he did." We read that those who heard and accepted the Christ were baptized, both men and women. Peter and John were sent from Jerusalem to check up on Philip's preaching. Philip did a fine piece of work which was accepted by the apostles.

The angel of the Lord appeared to Philip and told him to arise and go toward the south to the way that went down from Jerusalem to Gaza, which is unpopu-

58

lated. And he arose and went. He was a preacher of great faith. He might not have been able to understand all involved in the command, but he trusted that the angel was right, and he went. He was a preacher who was not preaching for popularity. He left a very successful meeting with crowds behind him and obeyed the Lord's leading. On the way he came to a crossroads. The Holy Spirit told him to join himself to the chariot coming in sight. The Holy Spirit could have informed the Ethiopian eunuch concerning Christ and redemption, but that duty had been left to men when the Great Commission was given. The Spirit worked through the preacher and today that Spirit works through the preacher and the written Word. The gospel is the power of God unto salvation, "with a man behind it."

Today the Holy Spirit operates through the preaching of the Word. Jesus said, John 6: 63, "It is the spirit that quickeneth; the flesh profiteth nothing: the words that I speak unto you, they are spirit, and they are life." The angel had no contact with the Ethiopian. His orders came to the preacher. The Spirit brought the preacher and the sinner together.

The man in the chariot was an Ethiopian eunuch, a man of great authority under Candace, the queen of the Ethiopians. He had been worshiping in Jerusalem and was now returning home. He was either a Jew or a Jewish proselyte. He knew nothing of the Christ or Christianity. He was an intelligent and an industrious man of prominence, and while riding along in his chariot he was reading from the prophet Isaiah. The place in the Scripture which he was reading was this statement from the prophet: "He was led as a sheep to the slaughter; and like a lamb dumb before his shearer, so opened he not his mouth."

Approaching the chariot in which was this man of high rank, Philip said, Do you understand what you are reading? And the reply was made, How can I except some man guide me? He then requested Philip to come up and sit with him in the chariot. The eunuch said to Philip, "Of whom speaketh the prophet this? of himself, or some other man?"

Here the sermon begins. "Philip opened his mouth, and began at the same scripture and preached unto him Jesus." Knowing what followed and knowing the text, one is not at a loss to know the body of that sermon. The man in the chariot was in the dark; he needed instruction. And the angel-sent, Spirit-filled man had the message. So beginning with that fifty-third chapter of Isaiah, Philip preached Jesus. He showed how Jesus fulfilled the Scripture, talked about His death on Calvary, and His resurrection.

Something was said in that sermon about baptism. That is not strange. How can any man preach the gospel and answer the question of his hearer when he asks what to do to be saved, and not say something about baptism. Baptism is included in the plan of salvation. Jesus said, "He that believeth and is baptized shall be saved." Paul said, "As many as have been baptized into Christ have put on Christ." Peter said in referring to the ark and the flood where eight were saved, "a like figure whereunto baptism doth now also save us." All the preaching in the apostolic days included baptism in the message. It was the last step one had to take in becoming a Christian. Faith changes a man's thinking. Repentance changes his manner of life. Confession presents his attitude toward the Christ and baptism changes his state. The angel-guided and Spirit-sent man delivering this message preached exactly what he had preached in Samaria when many believed and were baptized. He preached what Peter and John had been preaching when they gave their approval and confirmation of his work in Samaria.

This sermon was delivered in a conversational manner as the two rode along in the chariot. Many of the greatest sermons are preached when two people sit together and things are talked through. This is profitable personal work. Teaching now is a great need.

The Jews knew nothing about Christian baptism. In the old dispensation they had washings to cleanse them from defilement, from having come into contact with Gentiles. But that was not bapitsm in the light of New Testament practice and teaching. John's baptism was in order until Pentecost. Christian baptism began on that day and remains until this day.

When the Ethiopian's chariot rolled along and "came unto a certain water," the eunuch said to Philip, "See, here is water; what doth hinder me to be baptized?"

"A certain water" means a definite water, a place where water was continually. In the preaching Philip had stressed baptism as a necessity. Hence, the willingness of the Ethiopian to submit to the ordinance. One thing was required; namely, to measure up in the antecedents to baptism. Philip answered him, "if thou believest, thou mayest." The Ethiopian here made the good confession and said, "I believe that Jesus Christ is the Son of God." He acknowledged the creed of Christendom, the living, personal creed, the creed that needs no revision. Note here, there was no delay in rendering that obedience. He was not received on probation, nor was he told to wait until further instructions were given. They stopped the chariot and both went down into the water, both Philip and the eunuch, and Philip baptized him, and they both came up out of the water. Without controversy this baptism was a burial in water. Every place in the New Testament where Christian baptism is mentioned, it always means an immersion or burial in water. A preacher one time trying to substitute affusion for immersion stated that the Ethiopian was riding through a desert country where there was no water and he carried a jug of water in his chariot for drinking purposes, and that when Philip told him about baptism he brought forth the jug and said, "See, here is water." An old lady in the audience arose and said, "My Scripture teaches me that they both went down into the water. Therefore, are you trying to tell me they both went down into the jug and came up out of the jug." The old lady had more sense than the preacher.

In a New Testament baptism these things are to be noted: Water is used. They come to the water, they go down into the water, they come up out of the water. John was baptizing at Eynon near Salem because there was *much water,* which would not be necessary in sprinkling or pouring for baptism. Baptism is represented as a birth, a death, a burial, and a resurrection. In Romans 6: 5, it is called "a planting" and in Acts 22 and Hebrews 10 it is called "a washing."

In the obedience of the eunuch following his faith, he was a pardoned man. It is required that we meet the Lord where He has promised to meet us and He will then do all that he has promised to do.   In Acts 2: 47 it is stated that the Lord adds to the church those who are being saved.

Following this baptism, "the Spirit of the Lord caught away Philip that the eunuch saw him no more: and he went on his way rejoicing."   The eunuch rejoiced because he had a clear conscience.   He knew he had met the requirements of the Lord.   Christians should be the happiest people in the world.   They should rejoice for they are heirs of God and joint heirs with Jesus Christ.   The Christian religion is a singing religion, a happy religion.

The Ethiopian was now a Christian, a citizen of the kingdom of God, a member of the body of Christ, which is the church.

"PAUL'S EXHORTATION TO UNITY"

Ephesians 4: 3—6

"Keep the unity of the Spirit in the bonds of peace." Christian unity was a problem even in the days of the apostle. Jesus, as recorded in the seventeenth chapter of John, prayed for unity. He prayed for the disciples who were to become apostles that they might be one, sanctified to do the work whereunto He had called them. He also prayed "for those also which shall believe on me through their word; that they all may be one; as thou, Father, art in me and I in thee, that they also may be one in us: that the world may believe that thou hast sent me." This was the burden of His prayer before He left the upper room, crossed over the Brook Kedron and entered into Gethsemane with Peter, James, and John. The apostle Paul had a great deal to say about Christian unity. He, too, knew the day would come when the people would not endure sound doctrine. To Timothy, the young preacher, he wrote, "Take heed unto thyself and unto the doctrine." His first letter to the Corinthian church was a strong protest against division.

One of the tragedies in the religious world today is to be found in the divisions among those who would be followers of Jesus Christ. Christian men everywhere are coming to realize that there is weakness in division. Christ prayed that His followers might be one that the world might believe that God had sent Him. It is plainly to be seen that the divisions are a hindrance to the spreading of the gospel throughout the world.

During the apostolic age the followers of the Christ spoke the same thing. The apostles were led by the one Holy Spirit. Their messages rang true. The Spirit never contradicts himself. What is written, is written.

The union essential is the unity on the essential things, the things that are written, which need no interpretation, and no revision.

The pattern for the church of the living God has been given in unmistakably simple terms. The church is Christ's church, His body, His organization, of which He is the head, the King over His kingdom. In this fourth chapter of Ephesians, Paul sets forth the seven bonds of unity. He names various gifts that in that day were given to the church and names the offices essential for its edification. The unity of the Spirit makes for peace, which God will rule in the Christian's heart.

1. There is "one body." In Romans 12: 5 Paul said, "So we, being many, are one body in Christ, and every one members one of another." As in the human body there are many members, but all members have not the same function, but are essential to the perfect body, so, likewise, in the church the followers of Christ will have different gifts. Each one is important and each is expected to perform his duty to the best of his ability. Love is to predominate and is to be without dissimulation. The one body means the one church—Christ's organization on the earth. In Colossians 1: 18 Paul said, "And he is the head of the body, the church." The one body obtained through the apostolic age and on for some years to follow until the apostasy, when there was a gradual falling away from that which had been written. And ultimately we find another organization or body which, in

doctrine and polity, was far removed from the divine pattern laid down in the New Testament. That body was dominant until the dawn of the Reformation, when there was an attempt to reform the organization or body then in existence. That proving a failure, through the meeting of councils men departed from the body then so dominant, and in that separation, as time passed, there came into existence organizations known as divisions of the protesting or Protestant body. All of these were searching for the truth. They divided over many subjects, some essential and some nonessential. In the beginning of the last century the movement known as the Restoration had its inception. In Wales and in the United States men took the lead in calling people back to the old paths, to the restoration of the church in doctrine, polity, and life as the pattern is laid in the New Testament. In the United States there were many leaders, from many denominations, who sought to restore New Testament unity. Notably among these were Thomas Campbell and his son, Alexander Campbell, Barton W. Stone, and Walter Scott, with many others of like mind.

Christian unity is desired and is desirable. It also is possible. It is the popular subject under discussion today. The problem is how to obtain it. As of old, so today, "men do err, not knowing the scriptures." There is only one thing to do and that is to go back and proclaim the simple gospel and follow the design, the pattern of the church as laid down in the New Testament. Christ is the head of the church. The church is His kingdom and He is the King. It is a limited monarchy and He is the monarch. He has made the laws. These are not to be changed. Nothing is to be added to or taken from that which He has given. In all essential matters the Scriptures speak plainly. On the nonessentials, followers of the Christ can use their own judgment, but never are they permitted to make a disagreement on the nonessentials a test of membership in the body of Christ, the church.

2. "One Spirit." The same Spirit is bestowed upon Jew and Gentile and upon all the saints of God. The Holy Spirit never contradicts Himself. He is the agent which God uses in conveying His mind to the mind of men who have been selected to be recipients of the knowledge, who, in turn, being led by the Spirit into all truth, proclaimed the knowledge of God to men. That body of knowledge has been compiled into the book which we know as the New Testament. Today among the multiplicity of sects, each one claims to be led by the Holy Spirit, and yet in many things they go different ways. If all were being led by the Holy Spirit they would go in the same direction and walk together in peace and in love. The only way we can judge that one is being led by the Spirit is to see if his walk conforms to what is required and stipulated in the New Testament, for there is the place where the Spirit does His work today.

3. "Called in one hope." The one hope of all humanity who are called is the hope of immortality. That, too, is the great promise. Jesus said, "Because I live ye shall live also." He told the disciples He was going to prepare a place for them, that they might be with Him. The New Testament abounds in the promises of life eternal. Those promises take the sting and bitterness from tears that flow when death calls away a loved one. Paul had that glorious hope. And when the shadows of the

night of death were gathering, he wrote to Timothy stating that the time of his departure was at hand and that he was ready to be offered up. Having kept the faith, finished the course, and having fought a good fight, he was now assured there was laid up for him a crown of righteousness which the Lord, the righteous judge, would give him. Then he left this good word, "And not for me only, but for all those who love the coming of our Lord Jesus Christ."

4. "One Lord." The Lord is Christ, the head of the church. Paul said in 1 Corinthians 8: 6, "But to us there is but one God, the Father, of whom are all things, and we in him; and one Lord Jesus Christ, by whom are all things, and we by him." He will be crowned King of kings and Lord of lords. None will be superior to Him. "There is none other name under heaven given among men, whereby we must be saved." His name is exalted above every other name known to humanity. The one Lord who is the one King will reign over the one body, His church and His kingdom.

5. "One faith." The one Lord is the object of the one faith. That faith embraces the Christian system. Jude admonishes us to "earnestly contend" for the faith once for all delivered unto the saints. That faith is unchanging. That body of truth remains intact and stands like Gibraltar. There are not many faiths, but one faith, one system, as there is one Book, the one body, the one church, and the one Lord.

6. "One baptism." At the time Paul wrote this letter there was John's baptism, which was a baptism of repentance; there was Christian baptism, which is a burial in water of a penitent believer in the name of Jesus Christ,

for the remission of sins; there was also the baptism of the Holy Spirit, which had been given to the apostles to endue them with power and with knowledge and which had been given to Cornelius and his household as final proof that Gentiles had received the blessing and the sanction of heaven, giving them the privilege of being Christians.

The baptism in which all are concerned, therefore, is Christian baptism, intended for every individual who accepts Jesus the Christ, who will be buried with Him, and from that baptismal burial be raised to walk in newness of life. In that one baptism we put on Christ, for "as many as have been baptized into Christ have put on Christ." In that baptism preceded by faith, repentance, and confession, one receives the forgiveness of sins. Peter said to the people on Pentecost, who already had believed on the Christ, "Repent, and be baptized every one of you in the name of Jesus Christ for the remission of sins, and ye shall receive the gift of the Holy Spirit." Peter here is referring to water baptism. Apollos had come into Ephesus and preached John's baptism. Paul came later and corrected the mistake, rebaptizing twelve men who had been baptized according to John's formula. To show that this met with the approval of God, Paul laid his hands upon them and the Holy Spirit came upon them, and they spoke with tongues and prophesied. This was final proof that the baptism that Paul followed was the proper one. That conformed to the Great Commission, and is the baptism ordained in the Scriptures for this and every day until Christ comes. That baptism was a burial in water of a penitent believer in the name of Jesus Christ for the remission of sins. That is what

Paul means when he writes about "the one baptism."

7. "One God and Father of all." There are not many gods, but just one God for all people. Over the church is one supreme ruler, the God and the Father of all who believe on His Son Jesus Christ. From the above it is plainly seen that the points of unity of the church are: Unity of the head, unity of the Spirit dwelling in it; unity of hope; unity of faith; unity of ordinances for admission; unity of the one Father; unity of organization, one body. Let us walk in that unity, in the bonds of peace, loving one another. Then when the Christ comes, may He find His church without spot or wrinkle.

"JOHN, THE BLUE RIBBON MAN"

Matthew 11: 11

"Among them that are born of women there hath not risen a greater than John the Baptist."

This is a great compliment. In giving an appraisal of the life of an individual, we are concerned with whom it was who makes the appraisal. Compliments frequently are passed which are lacking in sincerity. We are extravagant with words.

The man who said that John the Baptist had no superior was not in the habit of passing compliments loosely or commending people. On another occasion while visiting in Syrophoenicia, He said to a woman in that country, "I have not found so great faith, no, not in Israel." When He was introduced to Nathanael, He said, "Behold an Israelite in whom there is no guile." That man was Jesus of Nazareth, the man of Galilee. He spoke discreetly, positively, and unmistakably.

The occasion on which He uttered the words of this text was an unexpected one. John had been cast into prison. He had sent two of his disciples to Jesus with the question, "Art thou he that should come or do we look for another?" Jesus replied, "Go and shew John again those things which ye do hear and see: the blind receive their sight, and the lame walk, the lepers are cleansed, and the deaf hear, the dead are raised up, and the poor have the gospel preached to them. And blessed is he whosoever shall not be offended in me." As the two disciples departed to make their report to John, Jesus said to the multitudes who were surrounding Him, "Among them that are born of women, there hath not risen a greater than John the Baptist."

John had heard in prison of some of the work that Jesus was doing. Why did he doubt? He had been a busy man. He was now shut off from the world. He who was known as "the voice of one crying in the wilderness" no longer was heard by the multitudes. Here was the man whom he had introduced to the world as the Messiah, and that man now was performing miracles. He had great power, but that was not being used in helping John's situation, hence the question, "Is this he or shall we look for another?"

John was a rare man in that he was an honest doubter. Many doubters are not honest. Bob Ingersoll was a dishonest doubter. Before his death, he said he never had read the New Testament with a desire to know the truth—he read it for argument's sake—to find something which he might hurl against Christianity. He admitted he knew nothing about the prophets. Had he read the prophets and then in the light of their statements read the Gospels, he would have said as it was said of old, "This is he concerning whom the prophets did speak." God knows the mind of man, its strength and its weakness. He desired His Son to be believed upon in the world. Accordingly, He gave the evidences which are sufficient enough to lead every man into the faith concerning the Christ. The facts have been presented, the evidences are here; but too often man is unwilling to consider them and therefore walks blindly. John was not of that type. A lonely, misunderstood, imprisoned man, a man acquainted with the great out of doors, did not permit his doubts to get him down. He called for more evidences and he received them.

John knew the prophets and remembered the picture painted by Isaiah, who said that the Christ would cause the blind to see, the deaf to hear, the lame to walk, and the gospel to be preached unto the poor. Jesus sent word back to John that that phophecy was being fulfilled.

John had an important mission. He was called of God and sent to preach in the wilderness. He had a great hearing and Jesus was brushing away any criticism of John. He assured the people that they had not been misled when in the wilderness they heard the mighty voice and submitted to the baptism which he gave.

John wrote no books, established no institutions. He had no press agents, no man-made auditorium in which to speak, no great papers to herald his presence, yet he was the mightiest preacher of his time. He was all preacher. He was not entangled with the affairs of the world, no pastoral duties consumed his time. An organization did not wait for his leadership. He was just a preacher, and Jesus said, "Among them that are born of women there hath not risen a greater than John the Baptist." To him was given the blue ribbon.

How great was John? There are different ways of measuring greatness. Men are great in various vocations and occupations and positions in life. Some are great economists. There are great statesmen, great men of science, great educators, great orators, great artists, and great poets. Every portrait is painted from a different point of view. John's status was not measured by the standard of a capitalist or a scientist. Jesus gave him pre-eminence as one who was spiritually great. Before

John came, in the long years that preceded him, there were many who were shining stars in the galaxy of the spiritually great. Call the roll of some of these: Abraham called from "Ur of the Chaldaeans" to become the father of the faithful, who could be tracked over Palestine by the altars he built. Moses—the emancipator of the Israelites, the lawgiver to Israel. Joshua, a great and good man in character and in faith and in works—the mighty warrior, a "plumed knight" of Israel, who after forty years of marching in the wilderness succeeded Moses and led the armies of Israel to victory when they entered Canaan. Samuel—the judge of Israel who had no marks upon his reputation, no stain upon his character. David, who on most occasions "behaved himself wisely," the king of Israel for forty years, a man who has given us rich devotional literature. Elijah, the prophet of fire, the hero of Mt. Carmel, the superintendent of the schools of the prophets. What shall we say of Isaiah the messianic prophet, Nehemiah, Ezekiel, and Amos, and a host of others! Look these men over. Take note of the mighty things they did, then stand along beside them this plain-spoken man John, who did not wear fine linens and fare sumptuously every day, but in long strides made his appearance in the wilderness in his garments of camel's hair, who sat down to his frugal meal of locust and wild honey. None of these men who preceded him were greater than he.

When Jesus passed the compliment upon John, several ideas undoubtedly were in his mind. The mother of Jesus was a cousin to the mother of John. Whether these men were acquainted before they met at the Jordan is not known. It is certain, however, that they knew of each

other. Jesus probably was thinking of that day when
having walked sixty miles from the home in Nazareth
cross-country to the river Jordan, where the crowds
were assembling in the wilderness to hear John, and to
be baptized by him in the Jordan that John, looking upon this spotless son of Mary, felt his inferiority and said
it was necessary that he, the baptizer, be baptized by
Jesus. There was no argument. Jesus merely replied,
"Thus it becometh us to fulfil all righteousness" and
John baptized him. The Holy Spirit coming as a dove
and the voice that came out of the heavens, saying, "This
is my beloved Son in whom I am well pleased," settled the
question for that day in the mind of John the Baptist,
who the day following pointed to Jesus and said, "Behold, the Lamb of God that taketh away the sins of the
world."

Jesus must also have had in mind the message that
John proclaimed in the wilderness. He said the kingdom
of heaven is at hand. He commanded the people to repent and be baptized. The baptism was a sign they had
repented. Jesus was concerned with the social order
which John was introducing. The conduct of the people was to be more than mere words, signing a card of
promise, or hurdling some ecclesiastical fence. There
stood in the wilderness a towering preacher like unto the
tall trees that "lift their leafy arms in prayer." Jesus remembered the throngs that came from Jerusalem, and
all Judea to hear this man of courage who was obsessed
with one idea, "to repent, for the kingdom of heaven is
at hand."

Jesus knew John to be a modest man, unselfish, not
a place seeker nor a social climber. When asked if he

were the Messiah that was to come, he said he was not, and that he was unworthy to loosen the sandals on the feet of the man that was to come. He declared himself to be "a voice in the wilderness" and declared that Jesus would increase but he would decrease.

It had been prophesied that he would be the introducer of the Christ and he would come in the spirit of Elijah. He and Elijah had some things in common.

Jesus thought of the time when John left the ease and the comfort of the good home and went into the wilderness away from the "crowd's ignoble strife." Whether he lived amid the noisy throng in the city or in the quiet of the wilderness, he wore the white flower of a blameless life. His preaching had such an effect upon the few that first came to hear him, that they must have gone through the country and announced his presence and thus helped to bring the multitudes within the sound of his voice. There in God's great cathedral, under the canopy of the heavens, this clarion voice sounded out like a bell calling the people to worship. To the multitude that heard Jesus say that no greater than John the Baptist had been born of women, He also went on to say, "What went ye out into the wilderness to see? A reed shaken with the wind? But what went ye out for to see? A man clothed in soft raiment? Behold, they that wear soft clothing are in king's houses. But what went ye out to see? A prophet? Yea, I say unto you and more than a prophet. For this is he, of whom it is written, Behold, I sent my messenger before thy face, which shall prepare the way before thee." John was no weakling. He could not be compared to a reed shaken in the wind. He was like the "Cedars of Lebanon" unshaken by the wind and whose roots spread deeply within the soil. John was unafraid in his speech. The truth of the Lord was his shield and buckler. He was not afraid "of the terror by night; nor of the arrow that flieth by day; nor of the pestilence that walketh in darkness; nor of the destruction that wasteth at noonday."

John rebuked the transgressors and sent his shafts of criticism at the hypocrites. The soldiers who mutinied because of the wages paid them by the Roman government were publicly addressed and told to be satisfied with their wages. All of this was new to that wilderness audience. He faced them like an "armed warrior." And like Him whom he came to introduce, he spoke with authority and the common people could understand him.

Doubtless, Jesus thought of that recent day when John was invited to mingle with society and to be the honored guest in the palatial mansion of Herod the ruler. Ordinarily, a humble preacher from the country would be somewhat embarrassed to sit at the table of a king. John was perfectly at home and carried with him through the palace doors his consecration. He asked for no quarters—he sought no favors. He was not a politician seeking office. There is nothing said about his complimenting his hosts on the quality of the food or the grandeur of their table. He was not interested in such things. But looking into the face of the woman at the table, and addressing the head of the house he said, "It is not lawful for thee to have thy brother's wife." This set the brain of Herodias whirling and she would have killed John, but she could not. Herod was fearful of John, knowing he was a just and holy man. John was cast into prison, but on a convenient day Herod had a birthday and invited his lords to the supper, and when the daughter of Herodias came in and danced before the crowd, the king promised her anything she would ask and her mother told her to request the head of John the Baptist. The king sent an executioner who beheaded John in prison and they brought his head on a charger and gave it to the damsel, who handed it to her mother. John lost his head in the performance of duty, but he did not lose his crown or his reputation.

John was born of good parents. His father, Zacharias, and his mother, Elisabeth, were aged people when he was born. The blood of fifteen centuries of priests ran in his veins. For fifteen centuries they had handled the holy things of the tabernacle and temple. All the way from Mt. Sinai up to the days of John the Baptist, they had been prominent in the work of Jehovah.

The religion that John found in his day was very largely a veneer. The Pharisees prayed to be heard of men. They had the letter but lacked the spirit. Their religion was a formal thing. John was spiritual, but he also called their attention to the practical side of the religion of Jehovah.

The field today is the world. An effectual and open door is before the preacher. To preach is a privilege, an opportunity, and a responsibility. The preacher must forget self and say, as the apostle Paul said, "This one thing I do." The field is white unto the harvest. We do well to imbibe the spirit of John the Baptist and preach the Word. Let us remember that the greatest compliment Jesus ever paid any man was paid to a rural preacher when He said, "Among them that are born of women, there hath not risen a greater than John the Baptist."

THE MYSTERY OF GODLINESS

1 *Timothy* 3: 16

To Timothy, a young minister of the gospel, Paul wrote, saying, "And without controversy great is the mystery of godliness: God was manifest in the flesh, justified in the Spirit, seen of angels, preached unto the Gentiles, believed on in the world, received up into glory." We live in a world of mystery. Everything in nature is mysterious. Mystery surrounds us in every direction. The natural laws in operation constitute a mystery. In the logical processes and the reproduction of life there is mystery. Like producing like is a mystery and in all the great variety of vegetation, flowers, and animal life we see mystery. The seedtime and the harvest—who can explain them? The radio, television, the airplane speeding across the sky—all are mysterious. We can not explain these things, but they are here; and we accept them, and understand they work in compliance with definite laws. None of these things are accidental. They have not come into being by chance. They are not the result of man's thinking and invention. Man simply has discovered the laws God has made. All of this we call a mystery.

Is it strange, then, that we find in the world of the Spirit much that is mysterious? Great facts mentioned by Paul as constituting "the mystery of godliness" can not be explained by man. This mystery God has revealed to us in the gospel, in order to make men godly.

1. "God was manifest in the flesh." That manifestation was made in Jesus Christ, God's only begotten Son.

Jesus said He came to make the Father manifest. Before Christ came, the world did not know God. He was recognized as a great power. He was looked upon as being fierce. He was not known to men as the God of love. They looked into the heavens with David and said, "the heavens declare the glory of God and the firmament sheweth his handywork." They saw the tornado sweep across the plains and said, "God is powerful." It remained for the Son of God to come to earth that in Him they might see the Father. When Jesus was asked by Philip to show him the Father, He replied, "He that hath seen me hath seen the Father." This does not mean God and the Son are the same, but it means they are alike. Jesus manifested to the world in human form what God would be if He, too, were to take human form. He revealed the Father to men. A lady from Pennsylvania, some years ago was driving through California. She stopped at a filling station, and to the young man filling her car with gasoline she said, "I knew a preacher in Ohio who looked exactly as you do. His name was Herbert Moninger. He died some years ago." The young man replied, "I am Malcolm Moninger, the son of Herbert Moninger." The young man was the manifestation of his father, he looked like his father. So when Jesus came, He revealed to the world what God the Father is like.

Jesus taught that God is love, and said, "God so loved the world, that he gave his only begotten Son, that whosoever believeth in him should not perish, but have everlasting life." Jesus said He was with the Father at the time of creation. John tells us: "In the beginning was the Word, and the Word was with God, and the Word was God." "And the Word was made flesh, and dwelt among us." All of this is a mystery but is revealed to us in the gospel.

2. "Justified in the Spirit." After His condemnation to death the power of God raised Jesus from the dead. Jesus made many claims while He was here. Some men doubted. All were not ready to accept Him as the Son of God. Some regarded Him as a mere man. Others said He was a prophet—a great teacher. Many rejected His claims when He said He would rise from the dead. His own disciples did not understand it. But all His claims were true. In the Holy Spirit, He was justified.

Many years ago two young men from Indiana, who had been looking for work in Missouri, were returning home penniless. They stopped at the home of a preacher by the name of Sweeney in Illinois. They told their story to Mrs. Sweeney, said they were sons of an elder in a rural church in Indiana. They were homeward bound, but were hungry, and were in need of something to eat and lodging for the night. The father was inclined to disbelieve their statement, but the mother invited them in, gave them their lodging and meals and the next day sent them on their way. A little later the son of that preacher, a young man named Z. T. Sweeney, went over into Indiana to preach in a village church. After the sermon of the morning, an elder invited him home for dinner. At the table sat two young men, sons of the elder. The boys said, "Are you the son of Elder Sweeney, minister of the church (giving the name of the town in Illinois)? Z. T. Sweeney replied, "Yes, he is my father." The boys replied, "When you return home, tell your father and your mother that you had dinner in the home of the elder whose sons were befriended by your parents as they passed their home some months ago." Z. T. Sweeney carried the message back to his parents and the boys had been justified.

Jesus Christ came, likewise, making great claims. They constituted a mystery in the minds of men. But in time the mystery was cleared. He was justified in the claims he made—justified in the Spirit. As Elder Sweeney was convicted of the righteousness of the two boys, so the world was convicted of the righteousness of Christ. He was justified.

3. "Seen of angels." An angel is a heavenly being, a messenger of God. Angels come in various forms. Any messenger of God may be called an angel. Christ was seen of the angelic beings who came from the courts of heaven, and He was seen by the human messengers of God upon this earth. Referring to the angelic beings from above, He was fed by one of them at the close of the temptation in the wilderness after He had spent forty days in meditation and communication with His Father. Angels were at the tomb when He arose from the dead. When He was cradled in the manger, wrapped in swaddling clothes on that lonely night in Bethlehem, angels sang the great anthem, "Glory to God in the highest; on earth, peace and good will toward men." God sheltered His Son, watched Him, sent angels to minister unto Him.

4. He was "preached unto the Gentiles." This was a fact most wonderful in the mind of a Jew like Paul, who had been trained to believe the Gentiles were accursed. When Christ came to earth and during His ministry, the Gentiles were treated only as dogs in the mind of the Jews, who held the position of being "the four hundred" of their day. It was difficult for the Jew to come to believe

that redemption through Christ was for all the world. To the Jew the Great Commission had its boundary. It was to reach no farther than the Jewish people. God's purpose was and is that whosoever believes on the Christ shall be saved.

The first Gentile conversion was that of Cornelius and his household at Caesarea Philippi, when an angel told Cornelius that his almsgiving and his prayers were recorded in heaven. He was then commanded to send to Joppa for a preacher by the name of Peter, who would come and tell him the words whereby he could be saved. That story is told in the tenth chapter of the Acts of the Apostles. Peter, taking six Jewish Christians with him as witnesses, preached the sermon. To convince those Jewish Christians that the Gentiles had the same privilege as the Jews in accepting the Christ, the Holy Spirit came upon Cornelius and his household and they spoke with tongues, which gave evidence that God had ratified what Peter had done. Peter turned to the six Jewish Christians and said, "Can any man forbid water that these should not be baptized who have received the Holy Ghost as well as we? And he commanded them to be baptized in the name of the Lord." This was the beginning of Gentile salvation.

5. "Believed on in the world." Here came a man born of plain people, whose cradle was a manger, reared in Nazareth from which no great man ever had come. His legal father was a carpenter and the boy worked at the carpenter's trade, was subject unto His parents, went to the synagogue to worship every Sabbath day and at the age of thirty unannounced, unheralded, He walked sixty miles across the country to where John the Baptist was

holding a meeting, and asked to be baptized, saying, "It becometh us to fulfil all righteousness." As John raised Him from the baptismal waters, the Holy Spirit fell upon Him, and God said, "This is my beloved Son in whom I am well pleased." Soon after He left the wilderness meeting, He went into the high mountains where for forty days He remained, and at the close of which He was tempted three times by the devil. But He won out in every temptation, came to Capernaum and began a ministry of a little more than three years, in which He went about doing good. And finally, in fulfillment of prophecy, He met death on Calvary. While His body lay in the tomb, His spirit went to preach to the spirits in prison. His spirit returned to that body and by the power of God He was raised. From time to time during forty days He met with His disciples, then ascended to the Father. They, ten days later on Pentecost, received the baptism of the Holy Spirit, began their ministry, being led by the Spirit to know the truth. Paul calls the fact that He was believed on in the world as "a mystery."

There are various ideas as to the claims of Jesus. Some said He was an impostor. He never acted like an impostor. Others said He was a tyrant. He was the personification of goodness, of mercy, and of peace. There was nothing tyrannical in His actions or His claims. Some said He was a good man, but was not the Redeemer. A Jewish rabbi said in a public address in Canton, some years ago, that the Jew today took off his hat to Jesus of Nazareth as a great ethical teacher, a good man, standing next to Moses in their estimation. But they could not accept Him as the Messiah. Jesus was more than a great teacher and more than a good man. He was divine.

He could not have been a good man if His claims were false. He made good in every claim. He never misrepresented, nor was He ever mistaken. There are three hundred thirty-three distinct messianic prophecies concerning Jesus. Every one of these has been fulfilled. The student of the Old and New Testaments, therefore, when he reads what was predicted, then beholds the fulfillment, exclaims, "This is he concerning whom the prophets did speak." The fulfillment of prophecy, the working of miracles, His resurrection from the dead, and His ascension above all the heavens to the Father leave no thoughtful person in doubt as to the deity of Jesus Christ. Men today are believing on Him in the world.

6. "He was received up into glory." Jesus said He would ascend to the Father on that never-to-be-forgotten day He met with His disciples, gave them the Great Commission, commanded them to go into all the world and preach the gospel to every creature. He had told them the Holy Spirit would come upon them and they should wait in Jerusalem until that day, and that the Spirit would guide them into all the truth. They were told that when in a tight place to have no worry or concern, for the Spirit would bring to their remembrance the things He had said. They were to be guided by the Holy Spirit. Jesus lifted His hands as if to bless the little group, then slowly was lifted up, carried beyond their sight. And as Peter tells us, He passed all the heavens, clear up to where God is. The disciples, rejoicing, returned to the upper room in Jerusalem and waited ten days for the coming of the Holy Spirit, when they began their mission.

Jesus the Christ stands today as our advocate, and our high priest at the right hand of God. When Stephen was stoned to death, he beheld the Christian's glory. Saul of Tarsus on the Damascus road heard His voice, and was overwhelmed by the light of His presence and there was called to the apostleship. That Christ lives today is not to be doubted. He now is our Saviour. At the consummation of all things He will be our judge. When it is all summed up, the purpose is well stated in the words of Jesus, who said, "I came that ye might have life and have it more abundantly."

WHAT THINK YE OF THE CHURCH?

"Ye do err, not knowing the scriptures, nor the power of God."—*Matthew* 22: 29

What think ye of the church? This question might will be asked of both the membership and the minister, but in this sermon we have another purpose. We plan to examine the answers so often given by men of the world—men who stay apart from the church and from the outside judge it.

One says, to the questioner, the church has the same standing as a club or lodge in his city. He can see no difference between the product of the church and that of the club or lodge. These organizations all have an altruistic purpose. He thinks they do as much good for humanity as does the church. These institutions stand for better things and in some instances outstrip the church in doing good. Thus Number One of our group outside of the church feels that the church has no mission, and therefore is eclipsed by the other organizations. Here he is in error, not knowing the Scriptures.

Number Two tells us the founder of church was only a man, not divine and not the Saviour of men. He does not believe that Jesus is the only begotten Son of God, questions His miracles, believes Him to be a good man who gave a fine system of ethics to the world, but that He is not the Messiah. Therefore, the church which Christ established is of no more importance in the world than any other organization which man has called into existence. Again, he errs, not knowing the Scriptures.

Number Three considers the Bible wholly the work of man's brain, and believes the writers of the Book had inspiration only as Shakespeare and all other writers had it. The statement of Jesus concerning the Holy Spirit being given to the apostles to guide them into all truth is not believed by this critic, for to him the Bible is only another book written by uninspired men. He is in error not knowing the Scriptures.

Number Four thinks morality is all that is required of men today. A professional man in Canton told me, "I have a religion of my own—'Do unto others as you would have others do unto you.'" That is one of the precepts of Jesus, but it does not embrace the full duty of the believers in Christ. Moral men are continually comparing themselves with what they see in Christian men and Christian women. Jesus said to Nicodemus that a man must be born again, born of the water and of the Spirit, and unless born again, he could not enter the kingdom of heaven. But the man of the street who disregards the deity of the Christ, will, of necessity, follow any human being whom he feels has the correct idea. He knows not the Scriptures.

The man of the street answers that the ordinances are not needed, that we have outgrown them and they are just things to remember. He doesn't regard baptism as at all essential to salvation. Not believing in the Christ as the only begotten Son of God, it follows anything Christ taught may be discarded at the will of these who stand on simply a moral platform and ignore the teaching of Him who said to the disciples as they were preparing to go forth: "Go ye into all the world, and preach the gospel to every creature. He that believeth and is baptized shall be saved; but he that believeth not shall be damned."

The Lord's Supper is, in the eyes of the man of the street, a needless institution. With him the death of Christ was of no effect and the Lord's Supper is a foolish memorial service in His memory.

Another, when asked, "what think ye of the church?" criticizes the membership for lack of interest. A Jewish rabbi in one of the large cities of this country, was invited to deliver an address at the banquet of a large number of Protestant ministers. He said, "If I believed what you men believe, I would not be at this banquet. Instead, I would be preaching 'in season and out of season,' warning, teaching, and, just 'as much as in me lieth,' attempting to reach the world with this gospel. If you believe in the divinity of Jesus of Nazareth, in the inspiration of the Bible, in immortality, and a heaven for the righteous, and punishment for the unrighteous, it would seem to me you should be on fire with the zeal of those early disciples, telling the world of these things and leading multitudes to an acceptance of the truth which you preach."

So, the world marvels at the indifference of Christian people with respect to their church attendance and devotion and support of Christian enterprise and the lack of much concern about the unredeemed.

Others say that by virtue of the love of God, none will be lost, that all are the sons of God, and will receive from Him a rich inheritance. Therefore, they ignore the church, which is the body, or the organization of the Christ, and they claim protection under the statement, "God is our Father and will have mercy." There are two errors here in not knowing the Scriptures. First, God is not the Father of every one. We read in the Gospel of John that "He came unto his own, and his own received him not. But as many as received him, to them gave he the power to *become the sons of God*." That Scripture makes it clear that only those who believe on the Lord Jesus Christ are sons of God. Jesus said to Nicodemus in John 3, "God so loved the world, that he gave his only begotten Son, that whosoever believeth in him should not perish, but have everlasting life." Here, emphatically, plainly, Jesus calls Himself the only begotten Son. All others who accept Jesus as the Christ have the privilege of being adopted into the family of God and will be known as adopted sons. To illustrate:

Here is a rich man in the community who has one son. He decides to adopt six boys who are without parents, are needy, and are willing to become members of his household. He goes to the probate court and adopts these six boys and they wear his name. His children now consist of one begotten son and six adopted sons. One day, he invites another boy to be adopted into his family. The boy refuses adoption, but accepts the invitation to live in the rich man's house, enjoy its comforts, and the fellowship of his son and adopted sons. He doesn't wear the family name; he does not recognize the head of the house as his father and the wife as his mother. The good man dies after a time. His will is read in which he states his estate is to be divided among his sons. The other lad who has been in the house almost as long as the adopted sons protests, asking why his name is omitted. The administrator asks him if he is the son of the deceased—do you wear his name? He replies that he was not adopted, that he did not take his name, but that he worked with the family, lived in the same house, ate at his table, had all the blessings which were given to his own children. Therefore, he claimed that his sojourn here in this fellowship and in this home entitled him to an inheritance.

No court in the United States would break that will. The difficulty is the eighth boy in that home was not the son of the man who died. The new boy who came in was not adopted—therefore, he is not included in the membership of the family. That is exactly the picture as it stands with respect to God being the Father of all men. He is the Father of all who accept Jesus Christ as His Son, and he is only the Creator by biological laws of those who reject the Son.

The man on the street can not understand the situation in which the church finds itself today. If he reads his Bible, he reads that Jesus prayed that the disciples might be one. He reads that Paul wrote the Corinthian church to "speak the same things," be of one mind, and that Paul likewise wrote, saying, "there is one body," which is the church. Today we have scores of denominations all having many truths in common, some teaching the traditions of men instead of the Word of God, thereby making the gospel null and void. The divisions among believers in the Christ are a hindrance to the ongoing of the church. It is a tragedy. The man in the street who knows anything about the Word of God can not see why the churches do not lay aside disciplines and creeds and many of the doctrines of men and go back beyond Augsburg, Nice, Constantinople, and Rome, and stand where the apostles stood in that early day, when Christians were bound into one brotherhood.

"WHEN THE CHRIST PREACHED IN PARADISE"

Luke 23: 43

"Today shalt thou be with me in paradise." These words were addressed by the Christ from the cross to the penitent thief who requested that the Lord remember him when He came into His kingdom. There are five facts which undergird the Christian system. They are the life, the death, the burial, the resurrection, and the ascension of our Lord. These facts have been well established. They are today beyond controversy. History proves that Jesus lived in the time and in the place which the Scriptures testified. He died. Those who crucified Him made a careful examination and said He was dead. Pilate accepted that fact. Two secret disciples, Joseph of Arimathea and Nicodemus, carried His body to its burial and laid it in the tomb of Joseph. The stone was rolled to the grave; it was sealed. The women who followed saw the place where they laid Him and hastened there as it began to dawn toward the first day of the week, that they might anoint the body, not knowing that soldiers were guarding it and the tomb was sealed. There is no question about His being buried.

The soldiers appointed to guard that body that no one might steal it hurried into the city and said that He had arisen. They were bribed to say His disciples had come and stolen the body while they slept. If they slept, they would not have known the body was stolen, nor who had taken it. If they had slept, they would have been put to death for that act. But not a hair of their heads was touched. They were paid the price, gave the lie. Christ was seen at least eleven times by men who had known Him well before His crucifixion. They had every opportunity of knowing this was He who had died on Calvary. They boldly went forth and proclaimed His resurrection. After He had spent forty days at different times with them, from their presence He ascended to the Father. In compliance with His request they tarried in Jerusalem ten days until the Holy Spirit came and endued them with power on Pentecost, when Peter preached the sermon testifying as to His death, burial, and resurrection, and won three thousand Jews to an acceptance of Him. The apostles baptized them on that day, which was the birthday of the church and the beginning of the kingdom of God upon the earth.

These facts are well established. The question now comes—while that body lay in the tomb, where was the spirit of the Christ? He said to the thief that He was going to paradise that day. But what and where is paradise? The word in the Hebrew means "orchard." In the Greek it is descriptive of a "park," "a beautiful place." It is three times used in the Hebrew of the Old Testament. Christ used it once as He spoke to the thief. Paul, in 2 Corinthians 12: 4, said he knew a man, doubtless referring to himself, who was caught up to paradise, and he also calls it "the third heaven."

The question now comes—why did He go to paradise? Peter gives the answer. In 1 Peter 3: 18-20 we read, "For Christ also hath once suffered for sins, the just for the unjust, that he might bring us to God, being put to death in the flesh, but quickened by the Spirit: by which also he went and preached unto the spirits in prison; which sometime were disobedient, when once the longsuffering of God waited in the days of Noah, while the ark was a preparing, wherein few, that is, eight souls, were saved by water. The like figure whereunto even baptism doth also now save us."

Jesus arose on the morning of the third day. Therefore, His spirit was in paradise preaching to those spirits in prison during that period in which His body was in the tomb. Those in prison were not there for punishment, but it was the waiting place for the coming of Him who was to preach unto them. Paradise, the third heaven and the prison, all refer to one state or place.

Next, this is written, that when Jesus ascended to the Father "he led captivity captive." Psalm 68: 18 says, "Thou hast ascended on high, thou hast led captivity captive: thou hast received gifts among men, yea, for the rebellious also, that the Lord God might dwell among them." In Ephesians 4: 8-10 Paul says, "Wherefore he saith, When he ascended up on high, he led captivity captive, and gave gifts unto men. (Now that he ascended, what is it but that he also descended first into the lower parts of the earth? He that descended is the same also that ascended far above all heavens, that he might fill all things.)"

This can mean but one thing—that the captives were those waiting in paradise for Christ's coming to preach to them. When He had done so, His Spirit returned to His body and by the power of God He was raised to walk during forty days with men, while the spirits in prison still awaited until His ascension. Then when He ascended, He led those in captivity whom He had captured, with Him, and they, too, ascended with Him.   While His body went into the tomb in the lower parts of the earth, in His ascension He went far above all the heavens, beyond the third heaven where paradise was, clear up to the top where God is and took with Him those whom He had captured.

Paul teaches in 1 Thessalonians 4: 14 that Christians are not to be ignorant concerning those who fall asleep, and that they sorrow not as others who have no hope.   He says those fallen asleep in Jesus will God bring with Him.   If this means anything at all, it means that the falling asleep applies to the body—the body sleeps, the Spirit lives.   Paul said, "To be absent from the body is to be present with the Lord."   This spirit never sleeps, but the body does.   In 1 Corinthians 15, Paul has a long exposition concerning the resurrection and life beyond. He there teaches that these fleshly, earthly, material bodies will not come forth.   He calls the coming back of the spirit a resurrection, because Christ was resurrected.   And he tells us that when Christ comes and the spirits return with Him, those spirits shall be given a glorified body fashioned like unto Christ's own glorious body.   The Lord is to descend from heaven.   He will have the voice of the archangel and the trumpet of God, and all those whose bodies have died, whose spirits have gone, will come forth with Him.   Then those living at that time will have their bodies changed in an instant.   And after those who returned with Him have come, we shall be caught up with them in the clouds and all together we shall meet the Lord in the air.   These words were given by Paul to the Thessalonians as a comforting message to those who were mourning.   These Scriptures answer some questions:

1. Do we have an intermediate-state body? Why should we have? What is the purpose of it? Christ isn't going into any intermediate state today to preach to any spirits awaiting His coming. His task of preaching the Christ to the world has now been committed to Christians, His disciples, who are commanded to "go into all the world and preach the gospel to every creature." Paul says that spirits absent from the body are present with the Lord. He is not now in the third heaven, where He went to preach to the imprisoned spirits, but in Ephesians 4: 10 it is said that He ascended *"far above all the heavens."*

The Roman Catholic church gets its idea of purgatory from this Scripture, teaching that the spirit here leaving the body goes into this place called purgatory—a place of purging—and the priest then intercedes in behalf of the departed spirit, providing he is paid well for it, and through his intercession the spirit is forgiven and released from this purging state. There is no such place and no authority for any such doctrine in the Scriptures.

2. Will the dead sleep until Christ comes? Those who have departed as in the days of Noah were not asleep. They had consciousness, heard Christ preach, were taught by Him, saw Him. There is no argument in the Scripture for soul sleeping. The body sleeps and wastes away, becoming a part of the common clay. Moses, who was taken to the top of Mt. Nebo nearly 1,500 years before Jesus was crucified, in company with Elijah the prophet, who likewise departed from this earth centuries before the coming of the Christ, came back and on the mount of transfiguration conversed with Christ, strengthening Him for the tragedy of Golgotha. They were living, conscious spirits, able to converse with the Christ

whose body was made glorious on the delectable mountain. Peter, James, and John were conscious of their presence and requested the privilege of making three booths for the three—Christ, Moses, and Elijah—and remaining on that mount. All of this is strong evidence that when the spirit of the Christian leaves his body, he is as conscious immediately after that instant as he was in the days before his body died. Because of this Paul could stand by the open grave and shout, "O death, where is thy sting? O grave, where is thy victory? . . . But thanks be to God which giveth us the victory through our Lord Jesus Christ."

This helps those who meet death, as it knocks at the door of loved ones, to face the tragedy heroically, for they have a glorious hope. And the loved ones, while absent in body, still live.

These Scriptures teach us that memory is undying. Christ one time said to the disciples that when they would appear before Him, He would remind them that when He was hungry they had fed Him; when naked they had clothed Him; in prison they had visited Him; thirsty, they gave Him to drink. And they would say, "Lord, we do not remember ever having done those things." Then He tells them that when they had fed others, clothed them, and rendered service in their behalf, that was credited as doing the same to and for Him. Memory goes beyond the grave. Having memory, it follows we shall have recognition. Anne Herbert has well said:

"When the mists have rolled in splendor from the beauty of the hills,
  And the sunlight falls in gladness on the river and the rills,
  We recall our Father's promise in the rainbow of the spray;
  We shall know each other better when the mists have rolled away.

Oft we tread the path before us with a weary, burdened heart;
Oft we toil amidst the shadows and our fields are far apart;
But the Saviour's "Come, ye blessed" all our labor will repay
When we gather in the morning where the mists have rolled away.

We shall come with joy and gladness, we shall gather 'round the
    throne
Face to face with those that love us, we shall know as we are known:
And the song of our redemption shall resound through endless day
When the shadows have departed and the mists have rolled away.

We shall know as we are known, never more to walk alone;
In the dawning of the morning of that bright and happy day,
We shall know each other better
When the mists have rolled away."

CALEB, THE MAN WHO WAS DIFFERENT

"But my servant Caleb, because he had another spirit with him, and hath followed me fully, him will I bring unto the land."—Numbers 14: 24.

This was the word God gave to Moses concerning Caleb. In Joshua, the fourteenth chapter, there is an account of Caleb holding a conference with Joshua concerning the division of the land. He represented the tribe of Judah. He called Joshua's attention to the fact that God had made the promise to Moses that Caleb, because of his faithfulness, would be brought into the land. He now came requesting that the mountainous country around Hebron be allotted to him and to Judah. He was now a man eighty-five years of age. He was forty when with the Israelites he left Egypt. He had had the long forty-year trek through the wilderness. He now was facing tasks that were to be performed only by one who was strong, possessing a good mind and a stout body.

It is quite probable that if Joshua looked at his good friend Caleb, he might have had some doubt as to his ability to meet the hardships that would come to one in the mountainous region. But to assure Joshua that he was able, Caleb said he was as strong and alert and capable at the age of eighty-five as he had been when he left Egypt at the age of forty.

Upon returning from the forty days in Canaan, forty-five years before this time, when the spies returned from having looked over the land, while ten said they were unable to possess it, Caleb with Joshua was optimistic and said, "We are able." In this interview with Joshua, again Caleb showed the optimistic spirit and gave the correct appraisal of his ability. It is quite customary for old men to admit the pressure of age upon their bodies. John Adams met by a friend on the streets of Boston one morning was greeted by the friend's question, "How are you this morning, John Adams?" The statesman replied, "John Adams is quite well, but the old house in which his spirit dwells will soon fall to pieces. The roof is not altogether what it was, the foundations are yielding to age, and in a little while this house that you now see will have fallen to pieces, but John Adams, the dweller therein, is all right." A week later he died in Washington City. He correctly estimated his strength and the inroad of the years upon his body. Caleb was different. He had lived right, he was used to hardships, and he was confident of his strength.

A few years ago Abe Corey, who had been a missionary at one time in China, met Bishop McDowell of the Methodist church, who also had been in China during the time that Corey was there. They were friends. Mr. Corey said, "Well Bishop, how are you?" To which the bishop replied, "Today I am eighty-four years of age. I can see as well as I ever did, hear as well, I can think better, and I can preach better than in former years; all of which I verily believe, but not a word of which is true." Caleb was different. He knew his strength and his power.

There was a reason for having selected the mountainous region around Hebron. There were associations that made Hebron a sacred spot. It was there that Abraham was visited by the angels who foretold the birth of Isaac to an aged man and his wife. The spies who had been sent into Canaan gathered the clusters of grapes from that territory and brought them back to Kadesh-barnea as a sample of what was raised there. From that point, Jacob sent Joseph from the ancestral estate to visit his brothers, who were watching the flocks at Dothan. It was from Hebron that Jacob and his sons and wives and grandchildren, eighty in number, climbed into the wagons and journeyed to Egypt when famine came over the land. Hebron was to the Israelites what Westminster Abbey is to the English and Arlington Cemetery in Washington is to the Americans. At Hebron were buried the patriarchs Abraham and Jacob and their wives with the exception of Rachel. It was the capital in which David ruled for seven and one-half years over Judah, before he established Jerusalem as capital of united Israel.

There was sentiment in the life of Caleb. Remove sentiment from any man's life and the charm and the music of that life is gone. We are all creatures of sentiment. Old men especially dream dreams and dwell very much in the past and their minds run back to the associations of other years. The home of one's ancestors is a sacred spot. The poet said:

> "As a hare whom hounds and horns pursue
> Pants to the place from which at first she flew,
> I still had hopes, my long vexations past,
> Here to return and die at home at last."

"As a man thinketh in his heart, so is he." The mind has a tremendous power over the body. The fact that Caleb thought he was able helped him, without any doubt, to be strong and to carry on. About the only good I can see in Christian Science is the fact that people are taught to think health. That is a commendable trait so long as it is not carried to too great an extreme. Physicians and psychiatrists state that a goodly per cent of the illness among people could be avoided if they thought right. Much of illness is neurotic. People can think themselves into illness and likewise into health.

Years ago a student in Hiram College had great fear that he might sometime have tuberculosis. His worry came to be a common knowledge among his friends. They agreed to call his attention to the fact that he was rapidly failing. During the day on the street, in the classroom, at the boarding house, and in his room, those who met him called his attention to how sickly he looked. To the first he replied he was perfectly well, but as the day wore on, he began to yield and by nightfall he was sick enough to go to bed. A student who owned a drug store in Mantua, a few miles from the college, was next to the joke and suggested to the student that he bring over to him the next morning a bottle of cod liver oil. In the morning the student was too ill to get out of bed so the cod liver oil was delivered. His friends had gathered near his room and after the druggist student had given him a large dose of the oil, they all broke in and gave him a laugh. Immediately he got over his scare and sickness, arose, dressed, went to breakfast and to class. One can think himself into most any condition.

Caleb was different. He knew himself, his powers, and was a man who could always say, "I am able."

> "If you think you are beaten, you are;
>   If you think you dare not, you don't.
> If you'd like to win, but think you can't,
>   It's almost certain that you won't.

"If you think you'll lose, you're lost;
  For out in the world we find
Success begins with a fellow's will.
  It's all in the state of mind.

"If you think you're outclassed, you are;
  You've got to think high to rise.
You've got to hustle before
  You can ever win a prize.

"Life's battles don't always go
  To the stronger or faster man;
But soon or late the man who wins
  Is the one who thinks he can."

Caleb was different in many ways. He was unlike the crowd which he helped to lead in the wilderness trek. He was optimistic when on the tour of Canaan. Spying the land, he saw the giants as did also the eleven others of the group. For forty days he studied them, saw their cities, and became well acquainted with their customs and habits. The people of Canaan were giants in the sight of the Israelites. Ten of the spies said they and their own people were as grasshoppers in comparison to the strength and size of the giants of that land. Caleb admitted that the men they met were strong, but with Joshua he stood over against the other ten spies and kept announcing, "We are able. We are able."

Caleb was not depending on human strength. He took God into account and with God's help he was sure of success.

Caleb was not afraid of majorities. He knew as we well know today that the truth does not always rest with the majority. Frequently the minorities are correct. When the ten succeeded in throwing fear and doubt into

the hearts of the Israelites, Caleb still stood his ground and
faced the entire wilderness people believing their ability
to win, provided they would let God lead them. It takes
a man of strong mind and spirit to fight against the majority.

Caleb was loyal to his God, to the leader, Moses, and
to the people. He never showed a white feather; he never joined in the criticism of Moses.

He followed God fully. It mattered not whether the
task was easy or difficult. He was always there to serve.
He never attempted to dictate to God, but when the going was hard and the people mutinied, Caleb stood like
the mountains around Hebron.

We have men of the spirit of Caleb in our churches
today. The pity is that all are not like Caleb. Caleb was
loyal to God and to the people. His example was always
for the good. Men to be of the mind of Caleb today
must, like the patriarch of old, follow God fully.

We can not dictate to God nor ask Him to change
His plans. To follow fully, people should be at their
place in the church and in the Bible school on the Lord's
Day; they should support the church financially according to their prosperity. They should be "fishers of men."
Too many people are spasmodic in their service and in
their worship. They go to church on Easter and any day
when great things are expected and crowds are to come
together.

The ones who follow God fully become an epistle
known and read of men. They go to church regardless
of weather conditions; they support their church financially; they pray not for themselves only, but for their
friends, for the church, and those who bear its burdens.

God has made a place for all such. He never breaks a promise and is within call every minute. Loyalty to Christ and following Him fully is well expressed in song and prayer, but is better expressed in action. Caleb came to the end of his days with no mark upon his reputation, no scar upon his character. He stands out as one of the shining stars in the galaxy of the great in the Old Testament world.

"ANDREW, SIMON PETER'S BROTHER"

"One . . . was Andrew, Simon Peter's brother."—John 1: 40.

We first met Andrew attending the meeting in which John the Baptist is doing the preaching in the wilderness along the Jordan River. He was a fisherman, the brother of Simon Peter. He lived at Bethsaida, known as "fish town," where other fishermen dwelt. Up until the time he met Jesus, he came and went unheralded, unsung. He occupied no great position in the community where he lived. He was just a plain, everyday fisherman.

He was acquainted with John and James, two other fishermen on the same waters. When John wrote of the great meeting along the Jordan and had occasion to refer to Andrew, the New Testament had practically been written. John's Gospel is reputed to be the last book written in the New Testament. Everybody who had read the Scriptures knew something about Simon Peter. Andrew had made no reputation for himself. He had done nothing which would bring a name to the front page of the papers. He played second fiddle in the orchestra.

When John told how Andrew had brought his own brother Peter to Christ, Peter had long since made a reputation for himself. He had been one of the outstanding apostles. To him had been given the keys of the kingdom. He had preached the great sermon on Pentecost, and had declared the deity of our Lord and the plan of salvation for all men to the Gentile household in Caesarea.

Now as John's natural force was abating and his eyes were growing dim and his hands trembling, he wrote his story concerning the Christ and to the people of his time, many years after Jesus had begun His ministry. John has occasion to refer to Andrew and simply introduce him by saying he is Simon Peter's brother.

This was a handicap to Andrew. Most men have overcome some handicap. Handicaps, when overcome, make one stronger, reveal determination, will power. Andrew's first handicap was that he had a great brother. No matter what he would do, he would be considered as one shining in the reputation of his brother.

John D. Rockefeller, Jr., one time said that he began life under a handicap—he was the son of a millionaire. He said his father had a good mother, but he, the son, had a mother just as good. His father had an excellent wife; he, too, was blessed with a wife just as good. His father had obedient and well-taught children; he, too, was not ashamed of his own children. His father began his career with $1.00 in his pocket, but he, the son, was endowed with a vast fortune as he put his feet on the first round of the ladder and started to climb. He declared it mattered not what he might do, and how successful he might be, the world would not give him much credit, for they would say, "His father was a rich man."

More is expected of sons and daughters who are the offspring of parents of renown. They seldom receive full credit for efforts of their own. The world says they should have done what they have done—look at the chance they had. They knew not penury or want. They were not called upon to make sacrifices. They did not have to climb the long stairway. They pushed the button and ascended in an elevator. So Andrew had been introduced to the world as the brother of a great man, Simon Peter.

Andrew did not permit the superiority of his brother to dampen his ardor or cause him to be envious, or to say, "It's no use." Andrew never imitated his brother Simon. We do not know that Andrew ever did much preaching. No sermon or address of his has ever found its way into print. If sermons he had, they long since have been lost.

Andrew was never an imitator—he was just his real self—plain Andrew. Imitators are soon discovered; they are cheap. Billy Sunday led in a union evangelistic campaign in Canton, Ohio, in 1912. Thousands of people hit the sawdust trail and accepted Christ in that campaign. After six weeks the meetings closed and Billy Sunday and his party moved on to another field. Some of the churches in Canton had follow-up meetings all the way from one to four weeks in duration. Two or three of those churches brought in evangelists to do the preaching to tie into the church those who had accepted the Christ, and now were to seek the church of their choice. The new evangelists, following the prince of evangelists, tried to imitate him. Some of them would throw off coats while preaching; others would stand on chairs, or frantically wave their arms in the air. And on the placards in the windows of the business houses in the city were to be seen their pictures, below which was their name, announcing "the second Billy Sunday." There never was such an animal! God made only one Billy Sunday. Imitators cheapened themselves and their message.

That was not characteristic of Andrew. Wisely, he just remained as he was. He never attempted to shine by reflected glory.

Andrew was a personal worker. He may never have preached a great sermon or swayed an audience by his eloquence. There is no record of any letters or books. He was the first to approach his own brother, Simon Peter, and take him to the Christ, who received him and gave the first indication that Simon Peter was to be one of the great men in the apostolic group. It is said of Andrew, "He first findeth his own brother, Simon, and saith unto him, We have found the Messias which is, being interpreted, the Christ. And he brought him to Jesus. And when Jesus beheld him, he said, Thou art Simon, the son of Jona; thou shalt be called Cephas, which is by interpretation, A stone."

Andrew began his personal work right where he was. He went to his superior brother, serving as the agent to bring him in contact with the Messiah. That was not an easy task. Many people who succeed quite well in reaching the sons of other people with the gospel, fail when it comes to persuading those of their own household. Andrew not only accosted Peter, but he brought him. He undoubtedly planned for a verdict.

Many a man today who is a good soldier in the army of Jesus Christ can trace his first steps toward the Master back to some friend who had the touch, the personal word and influence that induced him to become a Christian. Most people have to be discovered. Were it not for the fact that we have those who intercede for us and take an interest in us, many of us would be failures. One never knows what good may come from a sermon preached, a life lived, at the close of the day. In after years he may be startled when he sees the harvest of a few seeds that have been sown.

It is told that many years ago in Scotland the elders of a small church held a conference with their aged minister who had served them through a long term of years. They felt a young man should replace him, and in the conference reminded him there had been no conversions in the church for a period of a year. The old preacher replied, "Yes, there was one. Don't you remember, it was the wee lad, Bobbie?" They remembered the boy. Not only had he confessed Christ as his Saviour, but he had dedicated himself wholly to the Lord at a service held in the church in the interest of foreign missions. They remembered that it was this same little boy, Bobbie, who, when the offering plate was passed, asked the usher to place the plate on the floor. To the astonishment of all, the lad stepped barefoot into the plate and said, "I give myself to missionary service; it is all that I have to give."

The name "wee Bobbie" is not widely known, but his name as the gifted missionary in Africa is revered and loved the world over, among those who love his Lord, for this "wee Bobbie" was none other than Robert Moffatt. He became one of the brightest lights ever to shine upon the Dark Continent, only excelled perhaps by his son-in-law, David Livingstone.

When Andrew led Peter and introduced him to the Christ, little did he know the sermons Peter would preach and the people who would be helped by his preaching.

Andrew was not a quitter. He never sulked because he was not in the "inner circle." His brother, Simon Peter, and two other fishermen who were his neighbors, James and John, constituted that circle. They were the select with the Christ. He took them with Him up to the mount of transfiguration, where they beheld Moses and Elias. They were present when He raised the daughter of Jairus, and on that never-to-be-forgotten night, beneath the olive trees of Gethsemane, they went a little farther than the other eight, and were not far from Him when He sweat great drops of blood in prayer before the torchlight procession laid hands upon Him to lead Him to His trial and to death. That made no difference to Andrew. He was content just to be Andrew. Many an individual has been known to lay down the tools with which he worked, to throw aside the instrument upon which he played, to leave the choir in which he sang, to quit the church in which he worshiped, all because he could not have first place, or at least keep step with those who were in the limelight.

The great of this world, for the most part, began by taking a seat at the foot of the table. Later, they were given a seat at the right or at the left of the host.

Andrew was a good scout. He had an eye that was open, ever on the lookout for opportunities to do good. He did not wait for the fish to come to the spot where he was fishing—he went where the fish were. One day a multitude was assembled on the hillside listening to the great Teacher. The day had begun to wane. It was late afternoon and the people were hungry. There were no markets near, no inns, no place to eat. The disciples were in a quandary as to what to do with the hungry people. Andrew, in moving around among the people, found a little boy whose mother, in all probability, had prepared for him a lunch—five little loaves or biscuits and two little fishes. Knowing the power of the Master, he contacted the little fellow and led him to Jesus with all he had— his lunch. Jesus took the same, gave thanks, through

God's power multiplied it, fed five thousand men besides women and children, and at the close of that banquet the disciples gathered twelve baskets full that remained, that nothing be lost. Andrew did not perform the miracle. He did not bring the lunch with him, but he found the boy.

We need Andrews today in our churches. We need men who will look after boys. To discover a boy, teach him, have an influence over him, to be his guide, is a great privilege. Few boys would go to ruin if they had a good friend to encourage and help them day by day.

In 1851 a youth from rural New England was attracted to New York City and Brooklyn, the metropolis of the East. For a few days he wandered about the city seeking employment. From New York he went to Brooklyn and secured a position as clerk in a business house on Atlantic Street. One day on one of the bulletin boards he read an invitation to attend the Plymouth church, of which Henry Ward Beecher was the minister. He went. A year later he united with the church. The church was just four years old. The gentleman who stood at the door that first visit, acting as head usher, greeting people as they entered, shook hands with the boy, took his name and address, and during the week dropped into the place of business to become further acquainted. Sunday after Sunday as the lad sat in that church and watched the good man as he continued greeting the people, expressed the wish that he, too, sometime might have a like position. The time came when he became an usher and later was head usher, and for fifty-three years stood at that door greeting the thousands of people who entered for worship. That boy was Stephen M. Griswold, who,

when an old man, wrote the book entitled "Sixty Years
With Plymouth Church." Little did the man at the door,
who called to see and encourage the boy, think that here
was his successor, who would occupy the high position
for fifty-three years.

Andrew was that kind of man. If all our ushers today could be Andrews, the seats would be filled and the
people would enjoy coming to worship.

Andrew became conspicuous because of his service.
Every place we find his name he is in action, dealing with
people, helping somebody. He was like Abraham Lincoln's boy. A visitor to the White House asked the young
son of Lincoln where he might find his father. The boy
replied, "He left a little while ago for the railway station,
going to take the train and leave the city." Then he
added to the stranger, "When you go down to the station, if you see a tall man trying to help somebody, that's
my dad."

The story of Lincoln's son is quite different from the
story of another boy who, one chilly wintry morning,
was doing chores about the barn in his bare feet, standing first on one foot and then on the other. The preacher, new in that charge, came to the barn and said, "I am
the new preacher on this circuit, and I would like to see
your father." The boy said, "He's feeding the hogs over
in that hog pen—you'll know him, he's the one with the
hat on."

Andrew was the kind who always was helping people.
The Greeks came up to Jerusalem in those closing days of
Jesus' life, desiring to see him. They first came to Philip,
making inquiry, and Philip said, "I don't know where he
is." Andrew, hearing their request, took the Greeks and

soon found Jesus and introduced them. He could be known as "Andrew of the helping hand." He represents the great army of the middle class of humanity. We need men like Andrew and we need great preachers like Peter. Some one has said, "We need one great Niagara in this country, and we have it. We also need thousands of the little streams that go meandering through our valleys, emptying into the great bodies of water. They replenish the earth." So, likewise, a few great preachers may be needed, but we need the many, many thousands of lesser people who can be the light of the world, the salt of the earth, and have a helping hand for the community in which they dwell. God give us men, more men, of the character of Andrew!

HOW WILL YOU SHOW UP AT THE SHOWDOWN?

"Not every one that saith unto me, Lord, Lord, shall enter into the kingdom of heaven; but he that doeth the will of my Father which is in heaven."—Matthew 7: 21.

Jesus spoke plainly on this subject. The decision as to whether one shall enter into the kingdom of heaven or not depends upon his own choice. A man can not be a passive individual in this matter. He must act. "It is the Father's good pleasure that not one should be lost." "Whosoever calleth on the name of the Lord shall be saved." With his calling he must be willing to do the will of God.

"It is appointed unto all men once to die, but after death the judgment." Christ will be the judge of the quick and the dead. Judgment has been committed into His hand. No one questions death, and judgment is just as certain as death. The time to get ready for the judgment is now, for this is the only time of which we are assured. When the clock strikes the hour and the hour and the time of our departure is at hand, blessed is he who is prepared for that departure before the evil days come.

Pat lay upon his deathbed. The cold sweat was upon his brow. Impatiently and fearfully he awaited the end. His friend, Mike, entered the room and said, "Pat, don't be fearful. You will get justice." Pat replied, "That's just what I'm afraid of." So with many more! Jesus, in talking about the departure from this earth life, used the word "except" seven times showing that there were seven conditions any one of which could bar the gates of heaven against the soul's entrance.

In John 3: 5 he said, "*Except* a man be born of water and of the Spirit, he cannot enter into the kingdom of God." He was talking to Nicodemus. He was talking of the spiritual and not of the natural birth. To be born of the Spirit is to be begotten of the Spirit. Peter said, "Being born again, not of corruptible seed, but of incorruptible, by the word of God, which liveth and abideth for ever." Therefore, to be begotten of the Spirit the Word of God must be taught. One must believe what it teaches and believing comply with its demands. Upon obedience to it comes the promise of life eternal. One is begotten of the Spirit and is born of the water. Being born or begotten of the Spirit leads one to have faith and to repent and the birth in the water is the act of obedience. Baptism is a symbol of the birth. In all the evangelism of the apostles, who were the ambassadors of the Christ, they preached the Word, leading people to repentance following their faith, and then buried them in the water of Christian baptism and they were raised to walk in newness of life. There was no controversy about it. They were united in the one faith, obeyed in the one baptism, and served the one Lord.

"*Except* ye repent ye shall likewise perish" (Luke 13: 3). Repentance is the result of godly sorrow. Some feel bad because they are caught in sin and call that repentance. Repentance is bringing one's will into submission to the divine will. It is a turning around, a ceasing to do evil things and to do right. The prodigal son is a fine example of repentance. When he came to himself he resolved to go back to his father, confess his sins, and request that he be reinstated in the family circle although it be in one of the lowest stations. No one questions that we need to pray daily. Likewise, we are to repent continually. Repentance and prayer walking together bring one to the point where he is freed from condemnation. The truly repentant will also be much in prayer. One is baptized only once. The candidate having come to the age of accountability can call upon the name of the Lord and he can ask forgiveness and receive it.

Jesus said, "*Except* ye be converted, and become as little children, ye shall not enter into the kingdom of heaven" (Matthew 18: 3). The disciples were seeking prominent places in the new kingdom. The mother of James and John had interceded in their behalf. Belonging to the "inner circle," they felt constrained to make application for top positions, and they questioned Jesus, saying, "Who is the greatest in the kingdom of heaven?" Here He gives the answer. It is not the man of great knowledge or the man who occupies the highest place in public life or the one who has great possessions; but the man of true humility whom God honors. Jesus called a little child to Him and, setting him in the midst, said that it was necessary that one become as a little child in order to enter into the kingdom of heaven. Humility is one of the requirements—"Whosoever therefore shall humble himself as this little child, the same is greatest in the kingdom of heaven." Man is to be childlike but not childish. Children are no respecter of persons. They are teachable and humble.

In John 6: 44 Jesus said, "No man can come to me, *except* the Father which hath sent me draw him." To

Nicodemus, Jesus said, "No man can come unto me except the Father draw him." Jesus also said, "And I, if I be lifted up from the earth, will draw all men unto me." He was lifted up and His gospel is the drawing power. It contacts both the heart and the brain, the feeling and the thinking parts of mankind. Christ came to make God manifest. He said, "He that hath seen me hath seen the Father." By that, He meant that any one who had seen Christ had seen God, for God would do exactly what Christ was doing. Men are drawn by the gospel of Jesus Christ. That is why the apostles were commissioned to go into all the world and preach the gospel to every creature. That is why we preach today. The main purpose of all preaching is to make folk Christians.

It was a tragic hour. Jesus had preached to the multitudes. They were not accepting Him. In John 6: 53 he said, "*Except* ye eat the flesh of the Son of man, and drink his blood, ye have no life in you." The audience was surprised at that statement and all but the disciples left him. Turning to the little group that remained He said, "Will ye also go away?" Peter replied by saying, "Lord, to whom shall we go? . . . Thou hast the words of eternal life." Doubtless Jesus was thinking here of the memorial which He would establish later and did establish on that never-to-be-forgotten night in the upper room in Jerusalem, a few short hours before His crucifixion. He knew He would be lifted up upon the cross. He desired the disciples to remember Him, and on that last night before His crucifixion He took the loaf and blessed it and said, "This is my body"—meaning of course that it represented His body. Then the cup was handed to each one. They drank from it and He said, "This is my blood of the new testament, which is shed for many for the remission of sins."

In John 15: 1-4, Jesus said, "I am the true vine, and my Father is the husbandman. Every branch in me that beareth not fruit he taketh away: and every branch that beareth fruit, he purgeth it, that it may bring forth more fruit." Christ is the vine. Each individual believer in Christ is a branch. The branch gets its sustenance from the vine. The branch looks like the vine, it is composed of the same stuff, it bears the fruit, requires the pruning and cultivation. As it is essential for the branch to abide in the vine to be enabled to bear fruit, so it is essential for the disciples of Christ to abide in the fellowship of the Christ.

"*Except* your righteousness shall exceed the righteousness of the scribes and Pharisees, ye shall in no wise enter into the kingdom of heaven." Righteousness, when all the other requirements are met, can unlock the door admitting one into the kingdom of heaven. The scribes and the Pharisees were not very righteous. They were generous with the fruit of their toil, the vintage of their vineyards, and with the crops of their fields. There were those among them who entered into the letter, but not the spirit of religion. They loved to pray in public and on the street that others might hear them, and praise them for their much speaking. Their lives, which were being read by men, did not comport with their teaching. The righteousness which Christ expects of man results in right thinking and right living and measuring up the best of one's ability to all His requirements.

This is no easy task. It requires that one be instant in season and out of season.

All of this, and all of these statements made by our Lord, resolve themselves into this. One must become a child of God through the spiritual birth, and to use another figure, by adoption. One must have the spirit of repentance. He must be converted, which means to turn away from his transgressions, curb his desires, and walk in the new life. He must have an open mind for the teaching of God's Word, and the Word will draw him through Christ to God. The Lord's Supper plays an important part and occupies a conspicuous place in the program of the Christian. The Supper speaks a simple language which means, "Lest ye forget, Lest ye forget." It is not sufficient that one serve Christ today and then serve the devil tomorrow. The life that draws the prize is the one that is constant. Just as the branch that is attached to and abides in the vine, and from that vine draws sustenance, bears fruit, so the Christian must live in Christ and bear Christlike fruit.

"TRAIL'S END"

Deuteronomy 34: 5, 6

"So Moses the servant of the Lord died there in the land of Moab, according to the word of the Lord. And he buried him in a valley in the land of Moab, over against Bethpeor: but no man knoweth of his sepulchre unto this day."

Every trail has an end, be it traveled by a great or a small man. As a lullaby will be sung by a mother over the cradle of her babe, so, in due time, the funeral dirge for that same individual will be heard.

> "The leaves of the oak and the willow shall fade;
> Be scattered around, and together be laid.
> The young and the old, the low and the high,
> Shall molder to dust and together shall lie."

"Death has all seasons for its own." For each one the day will come when the silver cord will loosen and the golden bowl will break.

In this sermon there passes before the mind's eye a panoramic view of a great man—Moses, the lawgiver of Israel. His trail was a most interesting one. There is something more or less of importance about every trail. Dr. Oliver Wendell Holmes said that every man's life story, if well written, will have enough of interest in it to challenge the attention of him who will read. Nothing else in the world is of so much interest as the story of people. It is true, "The greatest study of mankind is man." This makes biography the most profitable and most interesting reading.

Trails are made by many feet, and they lead some-where. The Indian trails across the continent have now become the highways. Many interesting books have been written about trails. In this sermon we are following the trail of a great man—a man whom God chose to lead His people.

Moses was born in a home in Egypt where God was worshiped and a God-fearing mother rocked his cradle. Those were the days when Pharaoh ordered the death of the male children. God ever keeps watch over His own. It was in His plan that in the future day the people of Israel would be freed from the Egyptian yoke and would be set on their way to the land into which Abraham had come centuries before.

God began preparing for that event when Moses was born. The days of his babyhood and young childhood were spent in the home under his mother's watchful eye. He was then transferred to the palace of Pharaoh, where he was adopted by Pharaoh's daughter, who found him in the little basket among the reeds in the river, as she, with her maidens, came there to bathe. It was no acci-dent that day that little Miriam, the sister, was present at the right moment, and having taken the little babe from Pharaoh's daughter was permitted to find a He-brew woman, the mother of Moses, to care for him until he was old enough to be taken to the palace. Thus it is shown that "all things work together for good to them that love God, to them who are the called according to his purpose."

Nearly forty years were thus spent in the palace. Moses was educated above all the men of Israel, having had the best of training, but he never forgot the home

and the loved ones who dwelt there.   He was much like
the poet who said:

> "As a hare whom hounds and horns pursue
> Pants to the place from which at first she flew;
> I still had hopes, my long vexations past,
> Here to return and die at home at last."

This gives expression to the feeling each one has for the
days of childhood, the home and all of its happy memories.

On one of those journeys to his home, Moses encoun-
tered difficulty when he saw an Egyptian smiting a Hebrew, one of his brethren.   He slew the Egyptian and
hid his body in the sand.   The next day he saw two Hebrews striving together and he questioned the one who
did the wrong, asking why he was smiting his fellow.
The reply came like a stroke of lightning from a clear
sky, "Who made thee a prince and a judge over us? in-
tendest thou to kill me as thou killedst the Egyptian?"
This was the turning point in the life of Moses, for Pharaoh, having heard of the murder of the Egyptian, sought
to slay Moses, who fled and dwelt in the land of Midian.
Here he married Zipporah, the daughter of the priest of
Midian, whom he met as he sat by the well upon his ar-
rival in the wilderness.   He drove the shepherds away
who interfered with the seven daughters as they came to
draw water for their flocks.   Reuel, the father of the
girls, learning of the chivalry of the stranger, sent for
him to come to his house and eat bread.   The result was
the marriage to Zipporah.

The real schooling of Moses now began.   For forty
long years he followed the trail of the cattle and the sheep
through a wilderness trek.   It gave him a long time to

think and to meditate, to become acquainted with the
wilderness which must become the home of Israel in its
long journey to the land of Canaan.

God prepares men in various ways for the tasks He
has for them to perform. Many a life is influenced and
changed entirely by some small circumstance that took
place as they passed by. Influences are continually at
work on every hand which help to shape our destiny.

At the burning bush, Moses was called to go into
Egypt and deliver God's people from their bondage. His
alibis were all met. He was given miraculous power to
convince both the Israelites and Pharaoh that he was sent
of God. The shepherd's staff became a serpent and again
returned to be the staff. A man who spends forty years
herding cattle and sheep does not in that service improve
his oratory. Moses had the alibi that he was not a speaker and therefore would fail. But Aaron, his brother, was
given him to be his spokesman. Every obstacle was removed and the trail now leads back to Egypt to the homes
of the people and to the palace of Pharaoh. It was a
weary struggle, but Moses never lost heart. Ten plagues
came over the land before the hand of oppression was
lifted and Israel was commanded to leave.

The presence of God was made manifest in the bank-
ing of the waters of the Red Sea, and the passage of two
millions of people as they marched between the walls of
the water leading to the wilderness.

We now have a forty-year trail as Israel goes to and
fro before entering the land of their dreams. The trail
led them through experiences much like the experiences
of man in the world today. There were joys and sor-
rows, strength and weakness, faith and doubt, days when

the sun shone brightly and days when the clouds were heavy.

After the twelve spies returned, ten of whom gave an evil report concerning Canaan, people turned from Kadesh-barnea and spent the next thirty-eight years going to and fro. All above twenty years of age, except Moses, Joshua, and Caleb, died in that period. A new generation came on, many of whom had not known the rigors of life in Egypt. The manna was their daily food. The army became organized and moved with decorum and steady tread. Tears had been shed like the showers of the springtime when the fathers and mothers and many other members of the family were laid to rest. Thirty-eight years see great changes. The time now came when again Israel is given the opportunity of entering Canaan.

A new leader is needed, one whose ability makes him a general, a commander, a warrior. Who is better fitted for that task than Joshua? The trail now comes to an end. Moses was not permitted to enter the land, but viewed it from afar as he stood on Mount Nebo and beheld the promised land in all of its glory. One hundred twenty years of life had ended. The curtain falls, and the stage whereon Moses had played a great part was silent. The people watched him as the lonely figure took the path that led up to Mount Nebo. He did not return. He was buried, and God also buried his grave that no man knew the place of his burial. N. P. Willis wrote:

> "And had he not high honor?
>   The hillside for his pall;
> To lie in state, as the angels wait,
>   With stars for tapers tall."

There was no funeral service, no pallbearers tenderly to carry his body to its resting place.

On the plain below, when he did not return, the people mourned his death the customary length of time. When Joshua, his successor and understudy, was commanded to marshal the forces, the people were to prepare their food and within three days be ready to pass over the Jordan.

The long trail for Moses was at an end. He was a type of Christ, for he said, "A Prophet like unto me will the Lord your God raise up from among you. Him shall ye serve." "And there arose not a prophet since in Israel like unto Moses whom the Lord knew face to face." Through him the law for Israel was handed from God, and with his own hands he brought the tables of stone from Mount Sinai to the people assembled on the plain below.

Moses was a man of action—bold, courageous, and with a temper which, uncontrolled, led to an act which drove him from Egypt into the wilderness. And again, by his loss of self-control, he smote the rock in a fit of anger when told merely to speak to the rock that waters might gush forth to quench the thirst of Israel. That act revealed that Moses would not be adapted to the leadership required when Canaan had been entered. This was the cause of Joshua's being called to succeed Moses.

The trail of Moses is a type of the Christian life as set forth by Paul in the tenth chapter of 1 Corinthians, in which he describes the wilderness march and says, "Now these things were our examples, to the intent we should not lust after evil things as they also lusted."

We here have in this long trail the type and the antitype in this delineation. The type is as follows: The bondsmen of Egypt have their antitype in the sinners of the world. Egyptian bondage is a type of sin. Moses, the lawgiver and the deliverer, is the type of the Christ. The signs indicating that Moses was sent of God is a type of the miracles wrought by the Christ, which were His credentials. The message of deliverance finds its antitype in the gospel, which is for our deliverance. The faith that led Israel to act, is a type of faith which we have in our leader, the Christ. The turning away from Egypt is the type of our repentance when we turn away from sin. And being baptized into Moses in the cloud and in the sea is a type of our Christian baptism into Christ, His body, which is His organization, the church. The song that Miriam sang on the shores of the sea after the deliverance corresponds to the rejoicing of the Christian who is delivered from sin. And that trek in the long trail for forty years is a type of the Christian life. The Jordan lying between the wilderness and Canaan is a type of death—that stream across which each must go—lying between this land and the one over there. Canaan, reached at last, is a type of heaven to which we journey.

Ella Wheeler Wilcox sings:

> It seemeth such a little way to me:
>   Across to that strange country—the beyond;
> And yet not strange—for it has grown to be
>   The home of those of whom I am so fond;
> They make it seem familiar and most dear,
> As journeying friends bring distant countries near.

> So close it lies that, when my sight is clear
>   I think I see the brightly gleaming strand;
> I know I feel that those who've gone from here

Come near enough to touch my groping hand.
I often think but for our veiled eyes
We should find heaven right 'round about us lies.

I can not make it seem a day to dread
    When from this dear earth I shall journey out
To that still dearer country of the dead,
    And join the lost ones so long dreamed about.
I love this world; yet shall I love to go
And meet the friends who wait for me, I know.

I never stand about a bier and see
    The seal of death set on some well-loved face,
But that I think, 'One more to welcome me'
    When I shall cross the intervening space
Between this land and that one over there;
One more to make the strange beyond seem fair.

And so to me there is no sting to death,
    And so the grave has lost its victory;
It is but crossing, with abated breath,
    And white, set face, a little strip of sea;
To find my loved ones waiting on the shore,
More beautiful, more precious than before."

On the mount of transfiguration Moses reappeared, accompanied with Elijah to talk with Jesus concerning His death on the cross. The earthly trail of Moses ended on Nebo, but his spirit moved on. John was told on Patmos to write to the seven churches of Asia saying to them, "Blessed are the dead who die in the Lord from henceforth: yea, saith the Spirit, that they may rest from their labours; and their works do follow them." The works of Moses followed him. You can not bury a good man so deeply but that he will continue to sway the lives of those who tread over his grave.

William J. Clague, Minister